WHAT DO I DO WHEN
TEENAGERS ENCOUNTER BULLYING AND VIOLENCE?

Dr. Steven Gera

YOUTH SPECIALTIES

What Do I Do When Teenagers Encounter Bullying and Violence?
Copyright 2009 by Steve Gerali

Youth Specialties resources, 1890 Cordell Ct. Ste. 105, El Cajon, CA 92020 are published by Zondervan, 5300 Patterson Ave. SE, Grand Rapids, MI 49530.

ISBN 978-0-310-29194-7

Cover design by Invisible Creature
Interior design by Brandi Etheredge Design

Printed in the United States of America

09 10 11 12 13 14 • 20 19 18 17 16 15 14 13 12 11 10 9 8 7 6 5 4 3 2 1

CONTENTS

2.2 Questions That Demand Theological Consideration
2.2A Why Are People So Cruel?
2.2B Why Does God Allow Suffering?

2.3 Scripture Passages to Consider

SECTION 3: PRACTICAL ACTION TO TAKE WHEN BULLYING, VIOLENCE, AND AGGRESSION HIT A YOUTH MINISTRY 87

3.1 Duty to Warn

3.2 Prevention Strategies for Bullying
3.2A Preventative Program: The Youth Ministry's Responsibility
3.2B Identifying If Teenagers Are Being Bullied in the Youth Group
3.2C Empowering a Bullied Teenager
3.2D Transforming the Bully

3.3 Helping Disordered Teenagers

3.4 What If a Student Brings a Weapon to Youth Group?

3.5 What If You Receive a Bomb Threat?

3.6 Keeping Students Gang-Free

3.7 Protecting Your Students in Cyberspace

SECTION 4: RESOURCES ON TEENAGE BULLYING, VIOLENCE, AND AGGRESSION 109

4.1 Agencies

4.2 Online Resources

4.3 Books and Printed Materials

Notes 113

WHAT DO I DO WHEN...
BOOK SERIES
|INTRODUCTION|
Read This First!

It's very important you read this Introduction. This series of books has grown out of years of listening to professional and volunteer youth workers wrestle through difficult ministry situations. I usually know what's coming when the conversation starts with, "What do I do when...?" Most of the time they're looking for remedial help, but many times the issues that are covered in this book series have no preventative measures available. Many of these issues aren't given serious thought until they evidence themselves in the fabric of ministry. Then youth workers, church staff, parents, and even teenagers scramble to get some kind of understanding, remedy, support, or theological perspective on the situation. This series is designed to help you.

Before we move too far ahead, you need to know a few things. First, just because you read these books and acquire some helping skills, that doesn't make you a professional counselor or caregiver. In many situations you'll need to help parents and teenagers network with professional mental health workers, medical professionals, or, in some cases, legal counsel. Oftentimes the quality of care regarding these issues lies in the rapid response of helping professionals. So if you don't get anything else out of this series, get this:

The best thing you can do as an effective helper is realize you're not a trained counselor and you must refer, refer, refer.

Second, often when youth workers are in the throes of an issue, they'll quickly access the Internet for help and information. Researching something online can be very time-consuming, and it can provide unreliable information. So this book series is designed to offer reliable information that's quickly accessible for anyone who's working with adolescents.

Third, each book follows a similar format that's designed to help you navigate the information more easily. But more importantly, it also provides a model to help you deal with the issue at hand. What Do I Do When... books are divided into the following four sections:

SECTION 1: UNDERSTANDING THE ISSUE OR "PRESENTING PROBLEM"

Each book will start with an *epistemology* of the issue—in other words, the knowledge regarding its nature and scope. Many youth workers formulate their opinions, beliefs, and ideas using faulty information that's been passed through the grapevine—often without realizing the grapevine has root rot. Faulty information can change the trajectory of our actions in such a way it actually causes us to miss the mark. And many times our "misses" can be destructive to a kid who's already struggling with a painful issue.

We cannot expect to lead a teenager to the truth of Scripture if we start with a foundation that's built upon a lie or deception. We must be informed, seeking to understand the presenting problem as learners with a teachable spirit. In some cases these books may provide only the basics about an issue. But hopefully they'll be enough to create a solid foundation that gives direction for further research from reliable sources.

SECTION 2: UNDERSTANDING HOW THEOLOGY INTERSECTS THE ISSUE OR PRESENTING PROBLEM

Each book will also cover at least one theological perspective that informs the situation. However, please note I plan to give theological insights from multiple perspectives, so you'll know the theological voices adolescents and their families hear. Some of these voices may not resonate with your particular view, but it's important you develop a gracious, loving, and understanding heart. Keep in mind you're dealing with desperate, hurting, and broken people who—in the midst of their pain and struggle—are seeking grace and hope, not someone with theological answers.

I realize there's a danger in writing like this. Whenever the playing field is leveled—in other words, when one's internalized theological framework is challenged or an opposing theological view is given—it can quickly become a fisticuffs arena to champion truth. I believe that truth brings freedom (John 8:32). But let's remember that the Pharisees believed they'd cornered the market on truth simply because they held to a rigid interpretation of the Scriptures, yet they failed to listen for God's voice in others—especially in the Messiah.

A dear friend of mine once confronted a group of students by asking, "Is your interpretation of Scripture always right?"

The students knew that if they replied affirmatively, then they'd set themselves up as the source of infallibility. So they replied, "No, nobody can be right all the time."

My friend then asked, "In what areas are you wrong?"

His wisdom during that loving confrontation helped those students see that unless they openly and graciously engaged the theological perspectives of others, they'd never know if their own perspectives were lacking. Our goal in helping kids through difficult issues is to usher Christ into their situations. Many times that may not be with answers but with presence, affection, support, and understanding.

I recall a situation in which my dear, sweet, Italian mother was hurting for a young couple who'd been caught in sexual sin (she and my dad had mentored this couple). The disciplinary actions of the church were harsh and shaming. So while the church acted in rightness, it failed to see other theological perspectives that informed this situation, such as a theology of reconciliation, grace, confession, and absolution. In my conversation with my mother, I heard her engage these things because she, too, entered into the process and pain of this young couple, and she refused to apply a static template of dealing with the issue in a "right way." Instead, she decided to deal with the issue first in a loving and good way.

It's important to remember that many times rightness is not goodness. God has called his people to be good (Matthew 5:16, Ephesians 2:10, 1 Timothy 6:17-19)—not always "right." That doesn't mean we ignore truth, nor does it mean we minimize the authority of Scripture. It just means we must be incredibly and painfully careful to err on the side of that which is loving and good. Wrestling through various theological viewpoints, even if we don't initially agree with them, will keep us in the tension of being loving and good.

SECTION 3: CONSIDERING WHAT ACTIONS WE CAN TAKE

When we understand an issue or problem, we must wrestle through the theological and consider appropriate action. That can mean anything from doing more research to aggressively seeking solutions. In this third section, I'll attempt to provide you with a framework for action, including practical examples, applications, and tips. This will only be a skeletal plan you'll need to own and tweak to fit the uniqueness of your situation. There is rarely one prescribed action for an issue—every situation is unique because of the people involved.

Throughout the years, I've watched youth workers attempt to use books about youth ministry as one uses an instruction manual for the assembly of a bicycle. They assume that if they put this screw into this hole, then this part will operate correctly. Likewise, they expect that applying a tip from a book will fix a student or situation. If only life were this easy!

Every example provided in this series of books grows out of my years of ministry and clinical experience, input from God's people, and proven results. But they're not foolproof solutions. God desires to be intimately involved in the lives of students and their families, as they trust in God through their difficult times. There is no fix-all formula—just faithfulness. So as you follow some of the directives or action steps in these books, remember you must prayerfully seek God in the resolution of the issues.

SECTION 4: ADDITIONAL RESOURCES

In this section I'll provide some reliable resources for further help. These Internet sites, books, and organizations can assist you in mobilizing help for teenagers and their families. Hopefully this will save you many hours of hunting, so you can better invest in your students and their families.

Where needed, I'll also give a brief comment or description for the source. For example, some sources will serve to explain a different theological perspective from mainstream. This will help you to be informed before you run out and buy the book or engage the Web site.

I trust this book series will assist you in the critical care of teenagers and their families. God has put you on the front lines of attending, shepherding, and training people who are very dear and valuable to his heart. The way you respond to each person who's involved in these critical issues may have eternal consequences. My prayer is that everyone who reads these books will be empowered in a new way to usher Jesus more deeply and practically into the lives of precious teenagers.

UNDERSTANDING BULLYING, VIOLENCE, AND AGGRESSION

| SECTION 1 |

Susan, a high school sophomore, came home from youth group one Tuesday night. When asked how things went that evening, Susan announced to her mother, "I hate going there—and I don't ever want to go back!" Susan's family had been attending Christ Church since she was a small child. She'd grown up with many of the students in the ministry. As Susan's mother pressed the issue, Susan shared that one of the group's most popular girls told the other girls to exclude her from social plans, conversations, and relationships. She was being made fun of, talked about behind her back, and laughed at for her clothes, conversations, and idiosyncrasies. When her mother asked if she'd spoken to one of the youth workers about this, Susan replied, "Mom, what these girls are doing to me is so obvious; the youth workers just don't care." Susan wept over the pain she was experiencing.

Across town, Pastor Amy had just finished an outreach event at First Church. She was excited about the way the evening had gone until one of the students came running into the church to announce that a fight had broken out in the church parking lot. By the time Amy reached the lot, one of the visiting boys had pulled a knife on a core student and slashed his shoulder. In minutes the police swarmed the parking lot. The incident became the talk of the community. Parents raised serious concerns about "outreach events" and the types of kids attracted to those events. Amy spent months trying to "put out the fire" this single incident provoked.

The following morning, Jason, a senior who attended another high school on the other side of town, was driving to school with some of his buddies. Jason was active in the youth group at Community Church and a leader in his school. It had rained all night and large puddles of dirty water flooded the curbs on many of the streets. Jason decided it would be fun to drive fast and throw a wave of water over various students as they walked to school. He and his buddies got a great laugh out of the prank, and they drenched many students. This prank wasn't uncommon to Jason's form.

The common threads that run through each of these scenarios are the acts and effects of bullying and violence. Most youth workers would shrug off this issue, believing it's not something that hits their youth ministry. Yet every day countless numbers of teenagers are afraid to go to school and to youth group—anywhere their peers congregate, for that matter—because they've been victimized by bullying or violence. The implications of this means there may be students who come to church with their parents who won't come to youth group out of fear. Or it could mean there are many teenagers in our communities whose plight the church ignores out of ignorance. It could also mean there are countless students like Susan who endure the pain that erodes their personal sense of worth. For many, the long-term effects on their identities are devastating.

Youth workers work hard to make a youth group a loving community, but many times they're unaware of the bullying and violence that exists and runs stealthily among their kids. This problem shouldn't be taken lightly because it can be fatal for some teenagers. Bullying and violence are major concerns for youth ministry—not just in ministry to victimized kids, but also in the training of other students to be proactive against the problem. As you read this book, I trust you'll discover some preventative approaches, as well as some remedial methods, for dealing with this issue.

1.1 DEFINITION AND SCOPE

Bullying and violence are two sides of the same coin. In fact, the progression of violent behaviors often begins with some form of bullying. Verbal bullying leads to physical bullying, which leads to violence, which can result in a suicide or homicide—of either the victim or the bully (as a protective, defensive escape on the part of the victim).

You might be thinking, *That is so far removed from our youth ministry.* It's probably not as removed as you think. Teenagers who've been bullied feel as though other people are just disinterested bystanders who are watching their torment—just like Susan did in our opening story. If we don't come to the aid of hurting teenagers, then our teachings about Jesus' love and acceptance only fuel the fires of pain for bullied teenagers. They become convinced they're the unacceptable rejects. It becomes difficult for bullied teenagers to believe that Christ accepts them when his people stand by and watch them being tormented. This is why vengeful victims express their hatred for everyone, including Christians.

1.1A BULLYING

It is estimated that more than 30 percent (close to 5.7 million) of the teenagers in the United States are bullied or are bullies, or both.[1] It's more common for younger teenagers to bully or be targeted for bullying. As they grow older, this may lessen; but victims tend to remain a target even throughout high school. The repercussion of bullying on many of these students has long-term consequences into adulthood. While statistics indicate that 30 percent of all American teenagers encounter bullying, we must factor in that American culture is one of aggression and hostility. We teach our children to win. We champion aggression and power on the playing field, around the neighborhood, in the market-place, and even from our pulpits. Our entire corporate structure is built on the premise that aggressive actions make for success. We've divided aggression into categories of good and evil, and we wonder why children and adolescents don't discern this distinction more easily.

Therefore, due to these cultural attitudes and expectations surrounding aggression, much of the bullying among teenagers may be unreported and underestimated, which would lead us to conclude even more students are being bullied than statistics report.

In the movie *A Christmas Story*, we see the classic process of bullying as being comical. Ralphie Parker and his buddies, Flick and Schwartz, are constantly getting picked on by Scut Farkas and his sidekick, Grover Dill. These two torment the boys on their way to and from school each day. Yet, the movie passes it off as just an annoyance. Ralphie states, "In our world you were either a Bully, a Toady, or one of the nameless rabble of Victims." He quickly shakes it off and is consumed by other life issues (like securing an official Red Ryder carbine-action, range-model BB gun). If only it were that simple!

Ultimately, Ralphie gets his revenge when he finally reaches a breaking point and goes ballistic on Scut, punching and kicking and scratching him until Ralphie's mother breaks them up. Our society sees and portrays this as the solution. The message is those who bully can (it's fun), and the only way to stop being bullied is to be violent (it's applauded as heroic). Unfortunately, bullying has become more demeaning and painful today, and the means of stopping it more deadly.

Consider the tragic event that took place at Columbine High School on April 20, 1999, as well as a number of other school shootings. The forensics reveal that the shooters were victims of bullying who'd reached their breaking point. They became convinced relief could only be found through murder or suicide. They believed their final actions were heroic, as evidenced from a video Dylan Klebold and Eric Harris made months prior to their Columbine killing spree. The video "Hitmen for Hire" depicts Klebold and Harris as hitmen who come to the aid of bullied teenagers.

Journal clippings and other writings from these two boys revealed they were constantly feeling victimized. The Jefferson County Sheriff's Office in an official dossier, entitled *Columbine Documents*, recovered and released journal clippings from Eric Harris, which revealed he was constantly feeling victimized.

Eric Harris wrote:

If you pissed me off in the past you will die if I see you, because you might be able to piss off others and have it eventually all blow over but not me I never forget people who wronged me (entry dated 4/21/98).

If people would give me more compliments all of this might still be avoidable...probably not. Whatever I do people make fun of me, and sometimes directly to my face. I'll get revenge soon enough. F*@#&t% shouldn't have ripped on me so much huh! (entry dated 11/17/98).

I hate you people for leaving me out of so many fun things, and no don't f*@#%ing say "well thats your fault" because it isn't, you people had my phone number and I asked and all, but no no no no don't let the weird looking Eric kid come along (entry dated 4/3/99).[2]

Dylan Klebold wrote: "I swear—like I'm an outcast, & everyone is conspiring against me."[3]

Bullying really hit home for Christians in December of 2007. Matthew Murray, a 24-year-old alumnus of Youth With A Mission (YWAM), walked into their facility in Arvada, Colorado, and killed two students and wounded two others. Later that day he went to the New Life Church in Colorado Springs, killed two young women, and wounded three additional people before killing himself. This troubled young man had experienced rejection by Christians throughout his adolescence. Five years earlier he was denied going with students on a missions trip because of his instability.[4] This fueled his feelings of rejection at the hands of others.

Murray wrote:

If you're an extrovert, and popular, then yes, there is plenty of love waiting for you in christianity....If you ask questions and want to understand things and/or desire a real and deep spirituality, or if you're just not popular...well you are considered as one of the horrible people and are either going to be abused or kicked out by "holy spirit love filled" christians. it's all about the Beautiful People (entry dated 5/8/07; 5:34 P.M.).

He continues to indicate he is one of the "nobodies" saying, "How am I supposed to socialize and make new friends when I'm always left out of everything, and always made to be the outcast? I'm nice, I'm considerate, a lot of people tell me I'm intelligent and kind....so why the f*** must everyone think they have some right to abuse and reject me? (entry dated 10/31/07; 5:17 P.M.).[5]

Murray also borrowed Eric Harris' words:

I hate you people for leaving me out of so many fun things. Never inviting me to all your fun parties, never inviting me to hang out. And no, don't say, "Well, that's your fault" because it isn't. You people had my phone number, and I asked and all, but no no no no don't let the weird kid come along oooh f***ing nooo (entry dated 10/31/2007; 5:17 P.M.).[6]

Murray was so disillusioned by the response of Christians that he turned to an occult group for acceptance. There he found the same rejection he received from his Christian connections.[7]

One could argue there was more than just victimization involved in these tragic cases, that these were kids with severe psychological disorders. I would concede that this may be true.[8] However, questions still arise as to the epistemology of their disorders. Was it because they were continually bullied? Persistent bullying can lead a victim into deep depression, paranoia, and hopelessness. Could they have had the disorder without ever being bullied? Yes, but that doesn't merit shelving them and alienating them.

The Christian community needs to be a place where healing takes place. While we must protect the health and safety of our students, we shouldn't do this at the expense of marginalizing students who are unhealthy. If we feel we must exclude kids from an event or opportunity because wisdom merits it, then we must also make sure we go to great lengths to assure them they're loved and accepted. It's often easier to just ignore students who have issues. (In section 3 of this book, we'll discuss action steps for helping troubled teenagers.)

Bullying has been such a rampant and destructive force in teenagers' lives that the issue (often referred to as "adolescent victimization") has been addressed by organizations such as the National Education Association, the Congress, the American Medical Association, the American Psychological Association, the Centers for Disease Control, and the National Institute of Child Health and Human Development, as well as being researched among countless universities internationally and meriting the formation of many antibullying/antiviolence organizations—all recognizing the severity of this problem.

Since the year 2000, 16 states have passed legislation regarding school bullying. Those laws roughly define bullying and the victimization of children and adolescents; the behaviors that constitute bullying; as well as school and district policies prohibiting bullying and the communication of those policies to parents, teachers, and students. Yet the church seems to be silent on this issue. Youth workers must take a proactive stance against this beginning stage of violence, lest we find ourselves in the middle of a situation attempting remediation.

If we want to effectively help teenagers through this issue, then we must understand what bullying is. And by better understanding bullying, we can more easily recognize when teenagers are being victimized.

Below are some of the widely held views of what constitutes bullying. It's not a single incident. Bullying involves persistent actions over a long period of time. This relentlessness is what gives bullying its erosive power on the esteem, nerves, will, and patience of the victim. Kids who are bullied often wear a label of being weak or inferior and then they daily experience bullying. The label becomes so pervasive that regularly victimized people soon interpret every comment and action (smiles, glances, etc.) as threats.

Bullying is defined as—

- A person or group repeatedly attempts to threaten or harm a weaker, more vulnerable individual. There is a perceived imbalance of power, which gives an air of entitlement to one person or group to victimize another.
- A person or group constantly and willfully creates stress, fear, and terror in the life of a targeted individual or group.
- A random but serial behavior is carried out by someone who is feared.
- Unprovoked, deliberate, relentless, hurtful, persecuting, or aggressive behaviors are done to a targeted individual.
- A person or group physically picks on others, including shoving, hitting, pushing them around, and tripping them.
- A person or group continually makes someone the object of everyone else's joking or constantly laughs at or makes fun of that person.
- A person or group consistently delivers verbal threats, insults, racial slurs, name-calling, sexually demeaning comments,

taunts, or ridicule.

- A person or group frequently and deliberately humiliates others in public.
- A person or group continually rejects, isolates, avoids, and excludes a targeted person from social activity or relationships.
- A person or group makes frequent demands for money, personal property, or services, which are accompanied by severe threats if these demands aren't met.
- In some instances, such as when the physical and psychological well-being of the target is threatened, hazing is considered to be an aggressive form of bullying.
- In more aggressive cases, bullying involves violent behaviors, such as choking, stabbing, and assault.
- The intentional use of physical and psychological force or power, threatened or actual, against oneself, another person, or against a group or community that either results in or has a high likelihood of resulting in injury, death, psychological harm, maldevelopment, or deprivation (as defined by the World Health Organization of the United Nations).[9]

1.1B VIOLENCE AND AGGRESSION

The U.S. Department of Health and Human Services (USDHHS) stated in 2001 that, compared with other industrialized nations, adolescent violence in the United States is much higher and consequentially more lethal because of the use of firearms. According to the USDHHS report, adolescent violence is an epidemic and ranked as the second-leading cause of death among American teens.[10]

Adolescent violence involves any activity or behavior that's designed to inflict injury, cause damage, or deliberately interfere with someone's personal freedom and development. Violence and aggression by an angry or disillusioned teenager can be directed at others, self, or property (in cases of vandalism or arson).

Foundational work for understanding aggression was done by a psychobiologist named K. E. Moyer. Moyer studied the aggressive behaviors of people and animals, concluding that aggression can be defined categorically.[11] Moyer's categories help inform our understanding of teenager aggression:

Predatory Aggression: Attack on prey by a predator. This can be played out in the persistence of bullying. The bully or attacker singles out a target who becomes the object of the attacks. Bullies may stalk their victims or plan to entrap them so they can terrorize. Victims may fear particular locations (for example, corners, hallways, certain rooms) where the bully has ambushed them before or could ambush them in the future. Sometimes the victim may take long, out-of-the-way routes to get somewhere in order to avoid a possible encounter with the bully. Bullies may also go to great lengths to attack, terrorize, or humiliate their victims. These elaborate schemes mimic predatory behaviors.

Inter-Male Aggression: Competition between males. Fighting and usurping power over dominance, status, and ego become aggressive acts among adolescent guys. Guys are conditioned by our culture to settle their differences aggressively. Teenage guys are in a developmental age in which they're attempting to figure out their identities as men and as individuals. Autonomy and power are the two characteristics they perceive will move them from boyhood into manhood. Bullying, fisticuffs, and more aggressive means often equivocate power and status. (We'll examine gender differences in bullying later on in this book.)

Fear-Induced Aggression: Aggression associated with attempts to flee. We've heard of the fight-or-flight syndrome where, in the face of a threat and fear, people instinctually run, defend themselves, or both. This category of aggression provides insight on the retaliatory behaviors many bullied victims have resorted to using. When teenagers are persistently terrorized, they may eventually snap and strike back with irreversible consequences. Their pain and fear, along with a lack of sound judgment skills, lead them down a dead-end road where their only perceived option is to retaliate or die.

Irritable Aggression: Aggression induced by frustration and directed against an available target. Some believe teenagers who don't learn to manage their anger and frustration will become aggressive. This theory can be used to explain why an adolescent guy will punch a hole in a wall when he's angry, or why a group of girls will shoplift for the sheer rush of it. This also gives insight into why some teenagers bully or become violent. They feel frustrated with their quality of life or the number of stressors they're dealing with, and they take it out on a less powerful person. In that moment the rush of power and dominance gives them some sense of control they may not otherwise feel in their lives.

Spatial or Territorial Aggression: Defense of a fixed area against intruders. This is most notably seen in gangs, but it also plays itself out in behaviors provoked by relational jealousy in teenagers. Teenage girls who bully tend to display territorial aggression. They alienate their victims by physically or verbally pushing them out of a social circle.

Parental or Maternal Aggression: Aggression designed to protect offspring from threat or harm. While Moyer saw this as a defensive reaction of a parent protecting a child, we can categorically speak of the antithesis. When parents become overbearing and unreasonable, their behavior may provoke aggression in adolescents who are struggling to become autonomous, causing the teenagers to lash out at their parents. Some may argue that this category is no different from Irritable Aggression. I'd agree, but with the exception that the *parent* becomes the presenting and identifiable catalyst of the aggressive behavior. (We'll examine developmental reasons for bullying and aggression later in the book.)

Sexual Aggression: Aggression provoked out of sexual desire and sexual situations. This could include everything from jealous rage and sabotage to date rape and other sexual crimes. One example of how we see this played out is in teenage girls who become jealous of someone and spread rumors in order to alienate that person.

Instrumental Aggression: Aggression used to obtain some goal. This is a learned behavior among children and teenagers in which aggression is viewed as rewarding—fulfilling a need for power or obtaining personally desirable results. As a result, they bully because they believe it gives them respect and popularity.

1.2 VARIOUS FACES OF BULLYING, VIOLENCE, AND AGGRESSION

It's safe to say that more violent acts and acts of aggression are birthed in some form of bullying. Bullying is a form of aggression involving a perceived or actual imbalance of power and constant repetitive behavior against a target, over the duration of time. If the desired results of the bully aren't achieved, then bullying can become more aggressive or violent. If the bullying does achieve its intended response (fear, terror, pain, and so on), then the victim may conclude there's no alternative but to retaliate with heinous and irreversible violence. This conclusion is reached more quickly when teenage victims believe they're outcasts and nobody sees or is concerned about their plight.

We've already identified categories of aggression and defined *bullying*. But youth workers can feel impotent or lost when it comes to knowing what to do about bullying. When confronted, those teenagers who frequently bully others will often say they were only joking. And the victim may often concur with this story, fearing greater retaliation. This puts a youth worker in a difficult position of discernment, as teenagers tend to joke around by poking fun at each other. Some teenagers believe their actions are simple, lighthearted jokes (like Jason, the puddle driver described at the beginning of this book). But they cross the line when the joke is at the expense, harm, or humiliation of others.

Joking is some word or action that evokes joy and laughter. Many times this involves a target. We've all seen celebrity roasts, or we've had someone tease us about an idiosyncrasy, personality quirk, or some blunder we've made. We may have even been the object of a practical joke in which a prank was played on us and we all enjoyed a good laugh. So how do we differentiate between a practical joke and bullying? In order to discern the difference, we must create criteria that distinguish one from the other:

- Joking is a random, single event, as opposed to the *continual* fun that's derived at a targeted teenager's expense, over a long period of time. To ascertain the difference, a youth worker should ask how often and how long the joking has been going on.
- Teenagers cross the line of bullying when they cannot make fun of themselves as much as they do others, or if they cannot

be the object of others' jokes.

- If a teenager indicates to friends, confidants, or trusted adults that the joking hurts, then the actions have crossed the line into bullying. It's important to note that teenagers can be overly sensitive to joking or (in opposition) may not want to be perceived as being overly sensitive. In either case, the joking should cease. If it doesn't—it's bullying.

- If a teenager *never* follows joking with compliments or a kind word for the person who's the object of the joke, or if the jokester has little or no relationship with the targeted teenager except for that person being the object of the joke, then it's crossed the line into bullying.

- If a teenager isn't sensitive to how the targeted teenager may feel, if there's a lack of empathy, or if the joking takes an inappropriate turn (as in the case of hazing), then it can be considered an act of violence, aggression, or bullying.

Many times teenagers can be joking without realizing they're contributing to another person's persistent pain. Teenagers know and see when others are being bullied. Jokes that are made without an overwhelming amount of affirmation, declared value, love, and kindness contribute to the erosive effect of bullying. This is why bullied teenagers may see everyone as a threat.

1.2A FACES OF BULLYING

While we've looked at the broader categories and definition of bullying, it's important we identify the many faces in which bullying can manifest itself.

Physical Bullying: Younger teenage bullies begin by shoving, tripping, throwing things, hitting, and making obscene gestures at a victim. As the teenager grows older, he learns to make these physical actions more intimidating, humiliating, and aggressive. This means that physical bullying can escalate to punching, tripping, blocking someone's way, and provocations, such as bumping into the victim and making a scene, head slaps, flicking, or pinching. When these methods begin to lose their effectiveness, the bully may become even more physically aggressive, committing assault and battery, assault with a weapon, attempted murder, and sometimes murder.

Verbal Bullying: Many times a bully can't or doesn't bully without being verbal. Verbal bullying is damaging enough by itself, but its wounding ability is enhanced when accompanied by other faces of bullying. Many times girls will assault with just their words, while guys tend to assault others both physically *and* verbally. Verbal bullying can include name-calling, derogatory labeling, intimidating threats, gossip, slander, malice, rumors, obscenities and profanity, terrorizing phone calls, persistent ridicule and mocking, cruel jokes, and offensive noises.

Psychological Bullying: Psychological bullying is present in all other types of bullying, as it plays on the victim's emotions. The bully who uses fear, anxiety, terror, and so on as manipulative tools is engaging in psychological bullying. Emotional intimidation is the psychological bully's desired result, and it's accomplished by shunning, threatening, belittling, lying, manipulating, mocking, and attacking someone's personality, character traits, and idiosyncrasies. It attacks the victims' self-worth and esteem, making them feel helpless, out of control, devalued, inferior, hurt, afraid, and hopeless. While all bullying has a devastating psychological effect, girls tend to resort to psychological bullying more often than guys do. And they do so in a passive-aggressive role of manipulation, shunning, belittling, or malice.

Racial or Ethnic Bullying: Verbal, physical, and psychological bullying are all a part of racial and ethnic bullying. Kids who are bullied because of their race are often overlooked. We live in a society that values diversity and multiracial community on the surface. We seem to celebrate ethnic and cultural differences and teach our kids to respectfully embrace multiculturalism. However, when ethnically and culturally diverse teens retain their unique culture (i.e., accents, dress, foods, etc.) they become opportune targets for bullies, even in youth ministries.

A racial bully attacks physical and cultural differences by name-calling, making racial slurs, mocking, attacking a person's racial heritage, traditions, physical features, and so on. In addition, we've seen many ethnic groups integrate into a community. Students whose families immigrated to the area yet retain their ethnic heritage can become a target for bullies who attack speech accents, cultural dress, and a lack of knowledge about the dominant culture.

We must also be aware of intraracial bullying. This phenomenon is similar to the other types of bullying we've already examined, but it goes on *within* a racial group. A teenager may be bullied by others of the same race because of lighter or darker skin, physical features that do or don't match typical racial attributes, socioeconomic status, hair quality, intellectual ability, or material possessions. Victims of intraracial bullying are often overlooked because those in authority are seemingly ignorant of the person's culture and view the behavior as somehow ethnically appropriate. Therefore, these victims can end up feeling more devastated because they may already be part of a group that's in the minority in their community, and now they feel marginalized within that group as well.

Sexual Bullying: This face of bullying is often very difficult to separate from sexual aggression or assault. Most often sexual bullying can be defined as inappropriate comments and unwanted sexual touch. Some may ask if this is different from sexual harassment. The answer is technically no, not by definition anyway. The difference is that a sexual bully continually harasses his victim, whereas sexual harassment may be a single incident. Sexual bullying may involve demeaning comments about the victim's body or making the victim the object of a sexual joke.

Sexual bullying also includes "gay bashing." Many homosexual and transgender teenagers report being bullied, harassed, and even assaulted because of their homosexuality—almost three to four times more often than their heterosexual peers.[12] Students who don't normally bully others may participate in this because of their aversion to homosexuality. Regardless of a person's moral stance on the issue, bullying is an unacceptable response.

Another unfortunate thing about sexual bullying is that it targets those students who are only *perceived* to be homosexuals based on cultural stereotypes—for example, the guy who tends to be more effeminate or the girl who's more of a tomboy.

Virtual, or Cyber-Bullying: With advancements in technology, relationships and relational intimacy are being redefined. Additionally the cyber audience is much wider, far-reaching, and intentional. This gives a cyber-bully a greater number of available targets. The Pew Foundation found that girls are more likely to be victims of cyber-bullying than guys are, although guys are still cyber-bullied.[13] Late-adolescent girls reported being targets of cyber-bullying more often than younger girls did. Teenagers who use social networks such as MySpace are bullied more often than those who don't use them. When a comment or insult is posted online, its effect is lingering and compounded—often in a greater way than any verbal jab.

Cyber-bullies also persist in their bullying by sending threats; adding lewd or malicious comments; forwarding or publicly posting private emails or messages; blogging about rumors, lies, or gossip; and posting embarrassing pictures of the victim. Cyber-bullies often pose as someone else, concealing their true identity and then eliciting personal or sensitive information they can post. This cowardly act allows a cyber-bully to be nice to the victim in real time but act viciously in cyberspace.

This virtual bullying encompasses instant messaging, emails, comments posted on social networking sites and blogs, text messaging, and any other electronic messaging systems. With the availability of camera phones, cyber-bullies can also catch victims in embarrassing shots, which lock that victim into a moment in time. Cyber-bullies can create Web pages that are dedicated to victimizing. Some popular Web sites have even made cyber-bullying their business, allowing members to post derogatory or hateful comments and rumors about peers. Cyber-bullying can also include the omission of a positive response or the removal of someone from a friends list (also known as "unfriending" someone) on a social networking site.

Notes can be discarded, graffiti can be covered, but posts in cyberspace remain for long periods of time, often revealing a count of those who've visited the site. This ranks cyber-bullying among the most devastating form of bullying. Technically, any slanderous or defamatory statements that are put into print are termed *libel*, and the victim can take legal action against such behaviors. But the Web allows people to behave heinously and escape the responsibility for their actions.

More advancements are being made every day to uncover these acts of online libel. Teenagers who cyber-bully minimize the severity of it. They believe it's funny; therefore, they don't stop to consider the cost or consequence of their actions. They also believe they could never be caught, so they continue to cyber-bully others. Teenagers need to be aware they could be held legally and morally accountable for the things they post online.

Spiritual Bullying: Spiritual bullying can take the form of being persecuted for one's faith. Many teenagers may encounter verbal slurs or derogatory comments because of what they believe, but this face of bullying goes much deeper than that. Christians may spiritually bully other Christians. It's often done under the guise of calling out sin, but people are embarrassed, humiliated, and wounded at the hands of some well-meaning saint who champions the cause of "rightness." Many times this person doesn't even realize she's bullying someone. Yet, if you reread the definition of *bullying*, you'll find that these actions are just like those of classic bullies. In other words, they're exercising an imbalance of power and authority, being deliberately hurtful with their persecuting and judgmental behaviors, causing public humiliation, generating, an atmosphere of fear and dread, isolating and rejecting someone—and doing it all in the name of Jesus.

The apostle John mentioned a spiritual bully in 3 John 9-11. Diotrephes spiritually bullied the church by setting himself up as the preeminent leader (power); making false accusations; saying wicked things; and not accepting others but putting them out of the church instead. Diotrephes believed his behavior was justifiable, but John called it wicked. A Christ-follower's first and foremost response toward others should be loving and doing good, not seeking to prove ourselves right.

Now let's clarify something: I'm not advocating passivity toward sin. I'm saying I believe John gives us an appropriate response in 3 John: "Dear friend, do not imitate what is evil but what is good. Anyone who does what is good is from God. Anyone who does what is evil has not seen God" (v. 11). John is saying the primary focus of the believer is to be about doing good. If a confrontation is made, then it's done for the good of the individual—not to reveal rightness or a show of authority. If sin is confronted, then it's done so with careful consideration of what's loving and good, not with militancy and brazenness.

Spiritual bullying runs through our churches as a way of doctrinally positioning or separating ourselves from other denominations, religions, and the world. It's also often done in the church—and in youth ministries—to accomplish results. We bully people into conforming so we can count transformation. The sad part about this face of bullying is that it's often justified as God-honoring. Yet, when people come away wounded, humiliated, isolated, without the hope of reconciliation and redemption, and without seeing or experiencing goodness and love, then spiritual bullying has occurred.

1.2B FACES OF VIOLENCE
Violence among adolescents is a critical problem the church cannot ignore. To minister effectively to teenagers, we must

confront the evils that affect their lives. The Centers for Disease Control reported that 720,000 teenagers were treated in emergency rooms across America for violence-related injuries in 2006. In a 2007 survey, they also reported that 18 percent of teens admitted carrying a weapon to school in the past month, with 35.5 percent having been in some type of physical altercation.[14]

Teenagers are bombarded with images of violence in the media. Violence is sensational and dramatic, so it becomes the focal point of the news, the drama of our movies and television shows, and the tool for winning our video games. As a result, many kids perceive the world (neighborhoods, schools, and sometimes even church and home) to be an unsafe place. They carry weapons to protect themselves or, in some cases, to prepare for a preemptive strike, believing it's better to attack than be attacked.

Homicide is the leading cause of death among teenage African American males.[15] On the flip side, most all mass murders committed by a teen have been carried out by white, adolescent males. A juvenile mass murderer opens fire in a crowded public place with the goal of killing as many people as possible.

Violence is also on the rise among teenage girls, according to the U.S. Department of Justice and based on arrest records, victimization reports, and self-report surveys.[16]

Adolescents who engage in violent behaviors do so because violence—

- Gives them a sense of control, dominance, and power
- May be an act of desperation for a bully who moves on to more extreme behaviors to maintain his status and identity

- May be an act of desperation for victims of bullying to be free from the persistent pain that's been inflicted upon them
- May be viewed as a vigilante form of justice by a victimized teenager
- May be an attempt to gain respect
- May be an act of vengeance
- May be the result of adolescent immaturity compounded with other factors, such as alcohol, guns, and peer encouragement
- May be seen as the preferred mode of being accepted by peers (as in the case of gang involvement)

Violence among teenagers takes many faces:

Assault: Generally speaking, assault is usually considered a misdemeanor when the threat of physical contact is made by one individual with the intent to harm another individual. In some cases a threat made with the intent to harm given the gestures, intentions, and capabilities of the individual against a victim can constitute assault. Mere trash-talking or words designed to frighten an individual may not be assault—although it would be bullying. But if a teenager says he's going to beat someone bloody and then puts his fist through the wall or stabs his pen through the victim's picture—this may constitute assault. Students need to be aware that when they make verbal threats or comments in a fit of rage against someone, they can be held responsible for those threats as being acts of assault.

Battery: *Battery* is the legal term that involves physical contact and injury of an individual. The range of behaviors that constitutes battery includes everything from a slap to a closed-fisted beating. In many cases it's very difficult to separate assault from battery, which is why they're often coupled together. If separated, the act of battery is defined as the actual physical contact and injury brought upon an individual.

Aggravated Assault: This is a form of assault in which the intent or threat is murder, robbery, or rape. Aggravated assault is a felony. Assault with a weapon is also considered to be aggravated. Weapons commonly used by teenagers are guns, knives, baseball bats, and motor vehicles. Aggravated assault escalates when angry or provoked teenagers use drugs or alcohol. The availability of illegal substances and weapons to teenagers creates a deadly equation.

Sexual Assault: A 2005 survey of high school students found that 10.8 percent of girls and 4.2 percent of boys had been forced to have sexual intercourse at some time in their lives.[17] Adolescent girls between the ages of 16 and 19 are targeted for sexual victimization more than any other age group. An estimated 20 percent to 25 percent of college women in the United States experience attempted or completed rape during their college career.[18]

Sexual assault includes any unwanted or forced contact that is sexual in nature, such as inappropriate touch, attempted rape, acquaintance rape, date rape, gang rape, any forcible oral or genital contact, sodomy or object penetration, molestation, and incest. Sexual assault can also include any sexual threat, violence, or action that threatens the individual, such as voyeurism, exhibitionism, sexual coercion, and so on. (The topic of sexual misappropriation will be covered more in depth in another book in this series.)

Dating Violence: In a number of studies, between 20 percent and 50 percent of teenagers surveyed had experienced violence in a dating relationship. Girls are most likely to be punched, pushed or shaken, or forced into sexually compromising situations, whereas guys reported being pinched, slapped, kicked, or scratched.[19] Most of the time date violence is physical and emotional in nature, not some form of sexual violence that can occur in a dating relationship. (For the sake of this book, we've qualified that behavior as "sexual assault.")

Similar to spousal abuse, in acts of dating violence the victim is emotionally abused through threats, yelling, ridicule, and insults, as well as being physically assaulted or battered by their partner. The dynamic of this form of abuse keeps the victim and the aggressor in a relationship, which creates a cyclical pattern of abuse and enmeshment. The primary reasons dating violence occurs are jealousy and the need for power and control. Teenagers stay in these relationships due to feelings of insecurity (they believe they won't get another date), fear of the abusive partner, loyalty and even love for their partner, self-blame, and fear of social and legal repercussions. Many times teenagers are engaged in inappropriate behaviors (such as substance use, sexual activity, and they fear they'll be exposed if they report the violence.

Homicide: Depending on which survey you read, homicide is either the second- or third-leading cause of death among teenagers. This fluctuates depending on the specific type of group surveyed. For example, if we look at the general population of American teenagers, homicide is third behind suicide (second) and accidental death (primary). If we break this down by gender and ethnicity, the statistics change. Regardless, too many teenagers are dying at the violent hands of others. Gang involvement and handguns both increase the chances of homicidal death among teenagers. (We'll examine gang involvement and violence later in this book.)

> **Putting Things in Context**
> - If a teenager says he'd like to "blow up his math class because he hates math," then there should be little, albeit some, concern.
> - If the same student says he'd like to "blow up his math class because he hates all the students in it," then there should be great concern.
> - If he throws a chair across the room as he says either of the above statements, or if he has a history of violent outbreaks, then this could constitute assault.
> - If he says either of the above statements and is known to study Web sites on how to make a pipe bomb, or the materials for making a pipe bomb, are found in his possession, then this may constitute aggravated assault.

1.2C FACES OF AGGRESSION

Some teenagers exhibit violent behaviors that aren't targeted directly at individuals. These aggressive behaviors can still have dangerous or even deadly consequences. Teenage aggression has many faces:

Harm to Animals: Some teenagers take out their aggression by torturing, maiming, mutilating, and killing animals. These students often seek power and control by inflicting harm or pain over a creature less powerful than they are. This act may predispose an individual to abuse, destroy property, or harm other people. Many serial killers have engaged in this form of behavior prior to taking a human life. More than 40 states consider this sort of animal cruelty a felony. This behavior has become so closely linked to later criminal behaviors that many veterinarians have begun notifying authorities when they see suspicious cases. (They're not required to report unless they suspect organized animal fights.) The difficulty is that animal abuse is rarely done at the hand of the animal's owner (or the person who brings the animal to the doctor). Notification only makes the police more watchful.

Vandalism: This is the malicious and willful destruction and defacing of public or another person's property. Most vandals are adolescents who do it out of boredom, anger, revenge, or gang directives and identification. Vandalism includes spray-painting property; graffiti; destroying private property, such as mailboxes, windows, and landscaping; destroying public property, such as street signs, parking meters, and traffic lights; defacing and destroying public restrooms; or keying (scratching the paint finish) and defacing vehicles.

The Bureau of Justice Statistics reports that graffiti is the most common form of vandalism. Graffiti vandals are called "taggers." Most graffiti consists of gang symbols and signs. The majority of taggers are males between the ages of 12 and 21. Teenage girls account for only 15 percent of those taggers. Most juvenile vandals commit their crimes with a friend—they rarely do it alone. And one-third of all teenage acts of vandalism are committed while under the influence of alcohol. [20]

Theft: The law distinguishes theft, robbery, burglary, and larceny along the lines of where, how, and to whom the theft occurs.

Property Crime: The illegal taking or damaging of property, including cash and personal belongings. Examples include burglary, theft, robbery, and vandalism. In many instances, the offender acts furtively, and the victim isn't present when the crime occurs.

Larceny: The theft or attempted theft of property or cash without using force or illegal entry. An alternate label for this crime is "theft." It's a property crime.

Personal Larceny: Purse snatching and pocket picking. Personal larceny involves the theft or attempted theft of property or cash from the victim by stealth but without force or threat of force. It's both a property crime and a personal crime.

Robbery: The taking of property or cash directly from a person by force or threat of force. Robbery is both a property crime and a violent crime.

Burglary: The unlawful or forcible entry or attempted entry of a structure with the intent to commit an offense therein. This crime usually, but not always, involves theft. It's a property crime.

Theft is a violent behavior that involves the removal of someone's property for the express purpose of depriving that owner of it. Many teenagers engage in this aggressive form of behavior. The most common form of theft among students is shoplifting. Teenagers usually have the money to pay for the stolen items. And for teenagers who don't have the purchasing power, theft becomes a means of a quick status boost.

Teenagers steal for a variety of reasons, ranging from taking back control to feeling a sense of entitlement (even if they have the means to pay for it) to gaining status and respect from the material gain and from having defied the system to experiencing the sheer rush of stealing. And the stakes and value of the stolen items increase as a teenager gets older.

Teenage girls tend to shoplift more than their male counterparts do. However, teenage guys are convicted more often for robbery and burglary. Often these crimes are accompanied by other forms of violence, such as assault and battery, vandalism, and arson. Bullies tend to steal cash, iPods and other electronic devices, bicycles, food, clothing, homework—even gas (the victim may be forced to chauffeur the bully) and cell phone minutes (a bully may consistently take and use a victim's phone throughout the day).

Arson: This is the willful and malicious setting of fires. Arson is considered a violent crime against property and people. In 1994, the U.S. Fire Administration (USFA) reported that juveniles accounted for 55 percent of all arson arrests. According to the Office of Juvenile Justice and Delinquency, the arson-related arrests of juveniles were higher, proportionally, than for any other crime.[21]

The USFA identified two categories of teen arsonists. The first were emotionally troubled guys who express their negative emotions and feelings of powerlessness by starting fires. The second were delinquent criminal teenagers (predominantly male) who intend to destroy as an act of vengeance or power. The latter usually has a history of gang involvement, fire starting, substance abuse, and criminal activity. Juvenile arsonists tend to target schools, dumpsters near buildings, and abandoned buildings, to name a few, as the objects of their aggression.

Cutting and Self-Injury: This is violence directed at oneself. Many teenagers who self-injure do so for various reasons, including a need to be in control, the desire to escape or feel relief from emotional pain, a need to feel alive, a consequence of perceived worthlessness, or even punishment for everything from making mistakes to being who they are to atonement for their sin.

Forms of self-injury include cutting, scratching, burning, piercing, branding, pulling out body hair, and ingesting nausea-inducing or toxic substances. Self-injury can become an addictive behavior just like an eating disorder. Every time pain is inflicted, it creates an endorphin rush for the abusing teenager, which can induce everything from a sense of relief or numbness to a euphoric rush.

Most teenagers who harm themselves aren't suicidal. The majority of cutters and self-injurers are teenage girls, but guys who self-harm tend to be more violent in their methods. The following are some ways you can detect this form of aggressive self-abuse.

- Students may wear unseasonable clothing (such as long-sleeved shirts or long pants in the summer) to hide their injuries.
- They may be conscious that an injury may show, so they keep a grip on their sleeves or clutch the other openings of their clothes, such as the hems and necklines of their shirts.
- Parents find harm-inducing objects—such as razors, broken glass, box cutters, X-ACTO knives, a screwdriver or chisel, or other sharp objects—in their teenagers' rooms, drawers, under the mattress, and so on.
- Teenagers who burn or brand themselves do so by heating wires, paper clips, or metal objects with a lighter or candle. This paraphernalia is often hidden as well.
- Visible and unexplainable wounds, burn marks, or scars, particularly on arms, legs, and abdomen.
- The teenager frequently isolates herself in a locked bedroom or bathroom after a confrontation, time of stress, conflict, or whenever she's feeling negative emotions.
- The teenager begins hanging out with others who show visible signs of self-harm or evidence of other behaviors mentioned here.

- Teenagers who self-injure are unusually self-conscious about disrobing at camps or retreats when it comes time to sleep, swim, etc. They will go to extreme and unusual lengths to keep their body (arms, abdomen, legs, and thighs) concealed.
- Blood is found in bathrooms or bedrooms, or bloody objects—such as razors and glass shards—are found discarded in the trash or in unusual hiding places.
- Other teenagers or siblings give verbal cues, such as, "She has a bad gash on her arm," "He burned himself really bad," and so on.
- Infection and the symptoms of severe infection (fever, achiness, headaches, clammy skin, cold sweats, redness, painful swelling, pussy discharge, fatigue). To make matters worse, many teenagers who self-injure may interfere with the healing of their wounds by picking, continued cutting, and so on, causing infection to set in. Parents may discover discarded pussy or bloody bandages, clothes, or rags as well. This situation can become critical if medical attention isn't secured immediately.

Runaway: Running away from home is a teenager's dangerous and aggressive attempt to take control over his own life or to act in vengeance against parents or other loved ones. The Health Department estimates that more than 1 million teenagers between the ages of 14 and 17 run away from home each year. Teenage girl runaways outnumber teenage guys, three to one.[22] Many teenagers who run away will encounter additional problems such as robbery, molestation, rape, exploitation, beating, mugging, prostitution, and even death. Many engage in survival sex to meet their basic needs of food, shelter, and clothing. The National Runaway Switchboard estimates that at any given time there are about 2.8 million runaway and homeless teenagers living on the streets of the United States.[23]

So why do adolescents run away? Many times bullied teenagers perceive their parents as being disinterested in their lives because they believe parents should see the intense pain they're feeling and do something about it. Or they may believe their parents trivialize the severity of their issues. Bullied teenagers may also perceive the disciplinary actions of their parents as further bullying because they already feel controlled, dominated, and oppressed by their bullying peers. In addition, we should understand that many students can be victims of verbal abuse or bullying within their own homes. Therefore, a teenager often believes his only way of escape is to run away.

Typically, runaway teenagers only think through the "escape" part of running away but not the long-term consequences, implications, or dangers. Some teenagers meet friends online and then plan to run away to build a life with those friends. Their online friends seem accepting and engaging—offering a healing that teenagers desire. The cognitive immaturity of teenagers demonstrates a lack of foresight in discerning that the person they have been communicating with online is deceiving them. That cognitive immaturity coupled with the desperation the teenagers feel creates a dangerous equation that makes adolescents act impulsively.

Teenagers may also run away to the home of a friend or relative, or to a place where there is a safe adult—such as a youth worker. Second to these safe houses, teenagers run away to the promise of a job or career that ends up being a scam. Many teenage girls and guys (but predominantly girls) fall victim to sexual slavery because they run away to a promise they'll be turned into models or actors. The scammer lures them away by leading them to believe they're traveling to the location of a photo shoot or someplace where they'll be trained for this new profession. The teenager believes she's traveling to a safe location; but once she's trapped, she ends up far away from home. Other runaway teenagers find themselves spending nights on the street without food, shelter, and clothing because they've spent all their money executing their plan to run away and have no means to fix the situation or return home.

Some signs that precede a runaway are—

- Verbal cues about running away or leaving home
- Constant arguing about insignificant things
- Withdrawal or isolation
- Secrecy or acting strange

Disorders: The American Psychological Association has identified criteria for diagnosing teenagers with aggressive behavior disorders. A disorder can be defined as a pattern of emotional or behavioral problems that interferes with the teenager's ability to function in healthy or normal developmental and societal norms.

Teenagers who regularly engage in disruptive, aggressive, or violent behaviors may fall into one of two diagnostic categories: Oppositional Defiance Disorder (ODD) or a Conduct Disorder (CD). The following criteria are taken from the Diagnostic and Statistical Manual of Mental Disorders (DSM-IV):

Oppositional Defiance Disorder: To some extent we must first acknowledge there are going to be some teenage behaviors that are developmentally and age-appropriately defiant. Independence-seeking behaviors, strong wills, and a vast emotive range can be confused at times as ODD. As teenagers grow to be autonomous, they'll normally challenge authority. Therefore, it's important to note that diagnosing ODD is not an easy task, and it must be done by a mental health professional. Diagnosis often occurs when there's an ongoing pattern of defiant, disrespectful, and hostile behaviors on the part of the teenager that begins to affect family, academics, and social circles, or when it appears to be extreme when compared with the normal defiant behaviors of other teenagers.

Many times ODD is diagnosed when the pattern of defiance and hostility exists for more than six months and during which time four or more of the following behaviors are present:

- Often loses temper
- Often argues with adults (disrespectful, argumentative, and often verbally abusive and profane)
- Often actively defies or refuses to comply with adults' requests or rules (breaking curfew rules, skipping school, and so on; this can also escalate in defiance against the police, leading to arrest)
- Often deliberately annoys others (disrupts meetings, bullies, talks out of turn)
- Has difficulty maintaining peer relationships or friendships
- Blames others or circumstances for his mistakes or misbehavior
- Has academic difficulties
- Is touchy or easily annoyed by others
- Is often angry and resentful
- Is often spiteful and vindictive

The criterion is further met if these behaviors exist and don't occur exclusively during the course of a psychotic or mood disorder, such as post-traumatic stress or depression.

Conduct Disorder: This is a pattern of behaviors in which the rights of others or societal norms are violated. Unlike ODD, a conduct disorder takes the defiant behaviors to a different level. Defiance and hostility may still be present in a conduct disorder. However, the aggression is less likely to stop at attitude and mild behaviors, and it often escalates to inappropriate and dangerous behaviors.

The presence and severity of a conduct disorder is identified by onset, frequency, consistency, immediacy, and a number of the following criteria:

Aggression toward People and Animals

- Often bullies, threatens, or intimidates others
- Often initiates physical fights
- Has used a weapon that can cause serious physical harm to others
- Has been physically cruel to people
- Has been physically cruel to animals
- Has stolen something while confronting a victim
- Has forced someone into sexual activity

Destruction of Property

- Has deliberately engaged in firesetting with the intention of causing serious damage
- Has deliberately destroyed others' property (other than by firesetting)

Deceitfulness or Theft

- Has broken into someone else's house, building, or car
- Often lies in order to (1) obtain goods or favors, or (2) avoid obligations (in other words, the person "cons" others)

- Has stolen valuable items without confronting a victim (for example, shoplifting without breaking and entering; committing forgery)

Serious Violations of Rules

- Often stays out late at night despite parental prohibitions, beginning before age 13
- Has run away from home overnight at least twice while living in parental or parental surrogate home (or once without returning for a lengthy period)
- Is often truant from school, beginning before age 13
- Has clinically significant impairment in social, academic, or occupational functioning

Teenagers diagnosed with conduct disorders are often labeled as "delinquent," rather than having a mental illness. Most of the adolescents in treatment are there either because of family initiation, the suggestion of the teenager's school, or because of a court order due to a violation of the law. Many times a conduct disordered teenager evidences a *comorbidity,* or coexistence of another problem, such as mood or depressive disorder, anxiety, adjustment issues, learning problems, identity issues, and so on, along with the clinical diagnosis of having a conduct disorder.

The causes for these disorders aren't conclusive. They can include many things, such as the teenager's temperament, poor parenting, genetic predisposition, past and present abuse, academic pressure and failure, low self-esteem, mild brain impairment, and traumatic life experiences (in other words, parental substance addiction, divorce, frequent moves, and so on).

As with any disorder, treatment is a viable option to control or eliminate the problem. In the case of ODD and CD, successful treatment is time-intensive, difficult, and long-term. A teenager often views a counselor or mental health professional as an authority figure they perceive to be an oppositional enemy they should defy. Therefore, it takes time to build trust, break down barriers, and shift attitudes, before the real intervention can begin. After there's an established relationship, there are many treatment options, which include individual and family therapy, behavior modification programs that reteach proper coping and life-management skills for the teenager and proper parenting skills for parents, support groups, and, in some cases (such as when there are other existing issues such as Attention Deficit Hyperactivity Disorder (ADHD) or anxiety disorders) medical treatment may be introduced.

1.3 FACTORS THAT PLAY INTO TEENAGE BULLYING, VIOLENCE, AND AGGRESSION

The question often arises as to why some teenagers become bullies and use violent or aggressive means. We'll explore a number of answers in this section. All of them have valid and substantiated connections to the issue, but none of them has been found to be absolutely conclusive. This means cause-and-effect is not concrete, but there is some valid link between the problem and the factors. Some of those factors are as follows:

SIN NATURE

It would probably be remiss for us not to acknowledge right from the start that teenagers aren't exempt from the problem of evil. Out of the sinful nature of humanity, teenagers react to their circumstances with self-centeredness, pride, hate, anger, spite, power and control, aggression, violence, and abuse.

LACK OF LOVE

It may sound trite, but even nonreligious organizations have identified that teenagers who bully and remain violent later in life may be lacking a depth of love, affection, and positive regard. Many times this pattern of love depletion is traced back to their preteen and early childhood days. Family is the primary and most defining context in the life of a child. So if the family lacks the proper support and love for the individual, then that child (or teenager) may react inappropriately.

FAMILY DYNAMICS

There have been countless studies done on the cause and effect of family dynamics and environment on the development and behaviors of teenagers. Many variables have emerged that inform our understanding of teenage aggression:

Parents who are too permissive, unconcerned, or uninvolved. This allows the teenager to navigate life alone and unguided, yielding a trail of inappropriate decisions and behaviors.

Abuse and bullying modeled in the home. Teenagers begin to view this as the norm and reproduce the violent behaviors to get their intended results.

Authoritarian or punitive parenting styles. In these environments, discipline is often harsh, inappropriate, or threatening. Fear is often used as a motivator, so teenagers learn that fear can be used to manipulate others.

History of substance use and abuse. Families with a history of alcoholism or drug abuse often find there is genetic vulnerability toward these things. Teenagers may lash out in anger because of the anger that's heaped on them during an alcoholic rage.

Lack of proper role models. Some parents don't know how to control their rage and aggression. This is modeled as adult behavior for teenagers. Additionally, some teenagers are encouraged (by poor role-modeling parents) to be mean or cruel, to bully, to fight, and even to destroy other teenagers. This is venerated as proper one-upmanship.

Family history of mental illness. Violence and aggression can be a byproduct or symptom of some other mental health issue. Families with histories of ADHD, depressive disorders, or anxiety disorders may have teenagers who are predisposed to more aggressive behaviors if they experience these disorders. Additionally, if there's a history of violent and aggressive behavior in a family, it may predispose a teenager toward the same.

Marital discord. Much of the time discord in a marriage models attitudes, behaviors, and values of hostility, aggression, and oftentimes violence. Teenagers in this type of environment can feel insecure, hurt, anxious, and depressed. The hostility of the environment can breed hostile expressions of the pain and angst the teenager may be experiencing.

EXPOSURE TO VIOLENCE IN MEDIA AND VIDEO GAMES

Teenagers spend hours on end watching violence as a form of entertainment, and then they enter into virtual worlds where they can participate in the violence. Many organizations from the U.S. Department of Education to the U.S. Department of Justice have voiced concerns and cited studies about the effects of exposing children and teenagers to violence in media. Among the greatest concerns are the realism and gore with which violence is portrayed. Realism works to desensitize kids and create an unnatural familiarity with violence and aggression.

The majority of the studies done (more than 1,000) on violence and media since the popularization of television in the 1950s conclude that kids who are entertained by violence are more likely to exhibit violent and aggressive attitudes, values, and behaviors. In a joint statement made by the American Academy of Pediatrics (AAP), the American Psychological Association (APA), the American Academy of Child and Adolescent Psychiatry (AACAP), the American Medical Association (AMA), the American Academy of Family Physicians (AAFP), and the American Psychiatric Association (APA) at the Congressional Public Health Summit in 2000, these organizations proclaimed the following regarding the impact of entertainment violence on children:[24]

Children who witness a lot of violence are more likely to view violence as an effective way of settling conflicts. Children exposed to violence are more likely to assume that acts of violence are acceptable behavior.

Viewing violence can lead to emotional desensitization toward violence in real life. It can decrease the likelihood that one will take action on behalf of a victim when violence occurs.

Entertainment violence feeds a perception that the world is a violent and mean place. Viewing violence increases a person's fear of becoming a victim of violence, with a resultant increase in self-protective behaviors and a mistrust of others.

Viewing violence may lead to real-life violence. Children exposed to violent programming at a young age have a higher tendency for violent and aggressive behavior later in life than children who aren't so exposed.

LEARNING DISABILITIES AND POOR ACADEMIC PERFORMANCE
Some teenagers have learning problems that are never diagnosed. Their academic performance is blamed on apathy, lack of personal application, or poor discipline. The teenager's inability to correct the problem, along with the constant pressure to achieve, can create a defeated attitude that's often expressed in aggressive ways.

LACK OF "LIFE SKILLS" EDUCATION
Many adolescents lack knowledge and confidence in any type of conflict resolution or proper problem-solving skills. The quickest and most common way they learn to express themselves or handle their stress is through aggressive measures.

ACCESS TO FIREARMS AND OTHER WEAPONS
Aggressive or violent teenagers who live in homes in which a firearm or other form of weaponry is present are five times more likely to use that weapon in an aggressive way.[25] The availability of a weapon also becomes the empowering tool for a teenage victim to exact vengeance with a brutal show of force.

NEED TO BE ACCEPTED BY PEERS IN ORDER TO FIT IN OR FEEL COOL
Some teenagers get caught up in the culture of bullying or act

aggressively to get the attention of their peers. They perceive their actions and attitudes as a means of being accepted by others. Teenagers also mimic common attitudes and behaviors. Therefore, unless they're taught to be proactive about accepting bullied peers, they become part of the problem. This can often be played out in attitudes of superiority, disinterest, cutting comments, and so on. The other twist that must be considered is that some teenagers bully and act aggressively to protect themselves. The logic is that it's better to be on the side of the strong than the weak.

POVERTY AND DIMINISHED ECONOMIC OPPORTUNITIES

Teenagers who live in poverty and oppression can quickly spiral downward by defeat and feelings of being trapped. Lack of opportunities for work and furthering education breed a hopelessness that suffocates a person. Many times they believe the only option is to take what they need or aggressively seize control in order to break the cycle of oppression that binds them.

BAD COMPANY

Only a fool would believe that people's companions don't affect their attitudes, values, and behavior. Throughout Scripture we're reminded to keep watch of the company we keep. This biblical principle is also ingrained into the practices of nonreligious mental-health workers who include change of friendship circles as part of an effective intervention for troubled teenagers. Many teenagers develop aggressive lifestyles because of the people they hang out with. We already uncovered this phenomenon when we examined vandalism earlier in this book. This aggressive act is rarely done by a single individual. Vandals entertain themselves by being violent, and the audience is just as much a part of the experience as the destructive act. We'll take a more in-depth look at this when we examine the phenomenology of gang involvement.

1.4 GENDER DIFFERENCES IN BULLYING AND VIOLENCE

Significant studies have been done on gender differences regarding everything from tastes and desires to roles and perceptions. There have also been studies done on how teenagers of each gender respond, interact, and approach bullying and violence. All agree there are significant differences when the gender of a teenager is factored into the equation of bullying, violence, and aggression.

1.4A TEENAGE GUYS AND VIOLENCE, BULLYING, AND AGGRESSION

- Teenage guys are more aggressive in every way (work, play, whatever) than teenage girls. It's believed that testosterone affects the individual's aggression, and while some studies show this to be significant, there's no conclusive evidence that substantiates the truth of that claim.
- Teenage guys are more likely to use a handgun to assault a victim.
- More teenage guys have committed murders than teenage girls.
- Teenage guys who are bullied tend to act out in violent ways as a means of revenge or a solution to their own pain.
- Teenage guys who are relentlessly bullied believe their masculinity is so wounded that the only way they can recover their manhood is through extreme measures. By fantasizing about wiping out his enemies in a single act of vengeance, a teenage boy demonstrates himself to be powerful, feared, and forceful. Many times teenage guys are aggressive enough to follow through in making those fantasies reality.
- Teenage guys are more likely to take their own lives as a way to escape the torment and ridicule they experience. If provoked long

enough, they formulate the ideation they'll take as many people as they can with them, yielding murder-suicide situations.

- Teenage guys tend to be worse at reading emotional cues than girls are. This means guys may be hurt less by glances, gestures, and nonverbal cues than girls are. But it also means they may be more likely to misread neutral situations as being threatening.
- Teenage guys are wired to venerate their masculinity in acts of bravado. They demonstrate their manhood by toughness, interpersonal dominance, sexual virility, challenges of power and force, aggressive sporting ability, trash-talk, and so on. While some of this is acceptable, when it crosses the line, it can wound a guy's identity and lead to an aggressive attempt to recover his masculinity.
- Teenage guys tend to end up in more physical altercations than girls do, although this is rising among teenage girls.
- Teenage guys have been taught from the time they were little to fight back.
- Teenage guys fear being labeled weak, sissy, or effeminate.
- Teenage guys sometimes observe models of a spiritual man being direct, demanding, forceful, abrasive, and strong—men who spiritualize their bravado. Christian leadership is positioned in power, authority, intimidation, force, control, and hardness. Christian leaders model a "my-way-or-the-highway" rule, making the church a corporation and the senior pastor a CEO. This demonstrates to teenage guys that spiritual bullying makes a godly man. There's little room for meekness, gentleness, compassion, sensitivity, or kindness.
- Teenage guys (especially in America) are encoded with the message that real men don't surrender, and they rarely lose. This is why a guy will show up for a fight even when he knows he might take a beating. Or, more pointedly, he may show up to the fight with an arsenal ensuring he cannot lose.

- Teenage guys' brains develop differently from teenage girls' brains. The prefrontal cortex of a teenage girl's brain matures faster than that of her male counterpart. As a result, a teenage girl has better judgment skills than a guy does. He tends to be slower in calculating risk and danger and is more likely to engage in aggressive behaviors.
- In 2002, the U.S. Secret Service and the U.S. Department of Education issued a *Report and Findings of the Safe School Initiative: Implications for the Prevention of School Attacks in the United States.* After studying 37 incidents of targeted school violence (in an attempt to profile school attackers), the only common finding was that all of them were males.[26]

1.4B TEENAGE GIRLS AND BULLYING, VIOLENCE, AND AGGRESSION

- Teenage girls tend to develop relationships and identity in a hierarchical form. According to Rosalind Wiseman, founder of a national violence prevention program and author of *Queen Bees and Wannabes*, a "queen bee" is the ruler of a girls' clique or social group.[27] She uses her volition, money, looks, popularity, charisma, and reputation to manipulate the girls who want to be associated with her. The *Queen* is often also the group's controlling bully. In the hierarchy of the girls' clique, there's a *Sidekick* who serves as the bully's toady, being second in command; *Bankers* who gather gossip and use it to improve their status in the group; the *Torn Bystander* who knows the group is bullying and acting morally wrong, but doesn't do anything about it because she desires the group's acceptance; the *Pleaser/Wannabe/Messenger* who does the Queen's "dirty work" to feel important and stay in the Queen's good graces; and *Targets* who become the victims of the group's cruelty.
- Teenage girls who bully tend to bully only girls, whereas teenage guys bully both genders.

- Teenage girls tend to bully by spreading cruel jokes and rumors about the victim.
- Teenage girls are more likely to be the victims and the perpetrators of cyber-bullying.
- Teenage girls tend to use isolation, alienation, and relational aggression more as a means of bullying than their male counterparts do.
- Teenage girls who bully tend to be a part of a social network, do well in school, manipulate a group to participate in the bullying, and know the girl they're bullying. Whereas teenage guys who bully are usually socially awkward and inappropriate, have few friends, usually act alone, and target anyone they can overpower.
- Teenage girls are beginning to engage in more physically violent altercations, attacking in packs, slapping, punching, biting, scratching, and kicking their victims—sometimes to the point of unconsciousness.
- Most physical altercations with girls tend to be the result of gossip, romantic jealousies, looks, and status.
- Teenage girls' arrest rate for assault has increased over the last 20 years, according to the Office of Juvenile Justice and Delinquency Prevention, while arrest rates for assault among teenage guys has decreased slightly.[28]
- Teenage girls tend to be more violent in their homes (usually against their mothers), whereas teenage guys are more violent with strangers.
- A teenage girl's brain develops differently than a teenage guy's brain. Girls are able to read emotive data and are more affected by that data than guys are. A teenage girl can say something proper to another girl but do so while giving her a look that's destructive. This deceptive bullying tactic often allows a spiteful female bully to stay under the radar.

1.5 DEVELOPMENTAL TIES TO BULLYING AND VIOLENCE

Adolescence is an aggressive phase in the span of human development. A teenager's body, mind, identity, affect, temperament, and faith—in short, their total being—changes. This developmental era has been labeled by developmental psychologists as a time of storm and stress. Teenagers are making the shift from childhood to adulthood. Unless there are caring individuals to help them navigate the violent waters of adolescence along the way, they can be overcome and act out of the turmoil that marks their being.

Some of the primary developmental tasks teenagers must work through predispose them toward aggression. That means the developmental process has some built-in land mines that could lead a teenager to be aggressive. Before we go further, we should note that although these developmental land mines are present, the majority of adolescents don't act out violently. They may experience some form of aggression or rebellion, but not violence.

Additionally, it's important to note that just because there's a predisposition for aggression, that doesn't make all aggressive and violent forms of behavior acceptable. Teenagers are still developing a sense of morality and ethics. To ignore unacceptable behavior as a result of the growth process can actually impair another dimension of that teenager's growth. Let's examine some of these developmental tasks.

NEED FOR CONTROL AND AUTONOMY

Teenagers are moving from being dependent children to becoming independent or autonomous adults. This shift requires they understand when and how to be in control of their lives, circumstances, and relationships. This process is learned and practiced.

Teenagers who aren't coached or guided through this process may fall into bullying and other aggressive behaviors as a means to fulfill this developmental task.

It's also important to note that this sense of autonomy is what keeps victimized teenagers from seeking adults' help. These students feel trapped because they don't have the cognitive skills to work through the problem, yet they don't want to be perceived as a child by soliciting adult intervention.

NEED FOR PERSONAL POWER

Along with autonomy comes a need to have some power. If you have a conversation with a teenager about peer pressure, she'll most likely assure you she's her own person and not a product of peer pressure. That's because adolescents are attempting to establish their own sense of personal power. And while they aren't pressured, they are influenced.

Personal power is the way a teenager gauges how much he's influenced by and influences those around him. This internal-external jockeying for power is essential for teenagers to internalize a strong sense of ethics and personal value. When misguided, misunderstood, and abused, that natural internal empowerment can become a form of manipulation and bullying.

NEED FOR IDENTITY

Adolescence is the life stage during which individuals begin formulating their concepts about who they are. They must create an identity that's uniquely adult and gender appropriate. Girls attempt to identify themselves as adult women and guys as adult men. Because teenagers are taking on adult identities, they also attempt to engage in adult behaviors.

One such behavior involves the positioning of oneself in the social structure. This can be accomplished with anything from fashion to conversation. Comparing and contrasting oneself to the social landscape becomes the system of checks and balances on a person's social standing. This area alone can become a breeding ground for bullying and aggression.

Now if we add gender identity to the mix, we raise the stakes even more. From the time they're young, teenage guys are taught that in order to be a man they must—

- Be emotionally stoic and controlled
- Avoid shame at all costs
- Adopt a mask of bravado, which includes risky, aggressive, high-energy, and sometimes violent behavior
- Validate their manhood by their sexual prowess and their power or strength
- Never appear feminine, like a sissy, weak, or needy

As a result, this combination of traits and behaviors positions a teenage guy to become violent—which only serves to validate that he's a "man."

Teenage girls tend to be more relational and nurturing. We've already examined the relational pecking order a girl subscribes to. Her validation as a woman comes through her acceptance, love, and need to be needed by (nurture) others. This is why girls engage in greater relational aggression than guys do. But an interesting phenomenon has occurred—girls are beginning to adopt a masculine ideation of power. Girls are becoming more aggressive and physically violent toward others as a show of personal power. This type of behavior is perceived to be that of a "liberated woman."

1.6 PROFILES

Psychological studies have been done to profile victims, bullies, and others who'd act in aggressive or violent ways. In this section we'll examine some of those profiles. This may help youth workers detect if any of their students is a victim of bullying and violence or is engaging in inappropriate aggressive behaviors.

It's important to note here that these profiles are generalized, broad descriptions. They come after the fact, from compiled observations and psychological forensics. It's very difficult to create a concrete profile because both bullies and victims have engaged in violent acts. The U.S. Secret Service and the Department of Education attempted to create an accurate profile that would characterize a school attacker. Thirty-seven incidences of targeted school violence were studied in 2002 and "The Final Report and Findings of Safe School Initiatives: Implications for the Prevention of School Attacks in the United States" was released. Some interesting findings emerged about the attackers:[29]

- All were adolescent males between the ages of 11 and 21 (the majority between ages 13 and 18).
- They represented a diverse ethnicity: Caucasian, African American, Hispanic, Native Alaskan, Native American, and Asian.
- They came from a variety of family environments, but the majority were from two-parent, intact, community-involved families; a few came from foster homes with a history of neglect.

- Their academic records and achievements ranged from excellent to failing—the majority being categorized as good students.
- Their social relationships ranged from popular to isolated. The majority were considered to be mainstream teenagers who appeared to socialize with other mainstream teenagers.
- Two-thirds had rarely or never had disciplinary issues, while the others had experienced everything from a reprimand to an expulsion from school.
- Other variables examined were mental health issues, suicide ideation, and coping skills—all with the same varied range. There was no consistent mental-health profile that could serve as a signal for impending violence among these adolescent guys.
- There was no marked or dramatic change in the above-mentioned categories prior to the attacks.
- Three-fourths of the attackers were persecuted, bullied, threatened, attacked, or injured by others prior to the incident. On page 21 of this report, it reads:

> In several cases, individual attackers had experienced bullying and harassment that was long-standing and severe. In some of these cases the experience of being bullied seemed to have a significant impact on the attacker and appeared to have been a factor in his decision to mount an attack at the school. In one case, most of the attacker's schoolmates described the attacker as "the kid everyone teased." In witness statements from that incident, schoolmates alleged that nearly every child in the school had at some point thrown the attacker against a locker, tripped him in the hall, held his head under water in the pool or thrown things at him. Several schoolmates had noted that the attacker seemed more annoyed by, and less tolerant of, the teasing than usual in the days preceding the attack.[30]

Thus, an attempt to profile a student who may go on a violent rampage becomes an ineffective strategy for identifying teenagers who are at risk of committing mass violence in schools because the only common variable was gender. So in order to be more preventative, the Secret Service noted that it's more important for people who work with teenagers to keep a watchful eye on the behaviors and communications of adolescents.

Attacks on schools and churches are most often premeditated. Verbal cues that express plans, a desire to harm, and curiosity with violence (for example, making a bomb, or obsession with warfare or firearms) should be cause for alarm. This may also come out in the teenager's artistic expressions through morbid song lyrics, dark and disturbing stories, videos with violent themes, and artwork or doodling depicting violence.

Behavior is the second signal, which is hard to separate from the verbal because teenagers often talk to their friends and trusted adults about what they're doing. Teenagers who express their hatred, anger, and deep pain in aggressive ways become more of a concern when they go online and learn about building pipe bombs or practice shooting a firearm without adult supervision or knowledge.

The most common mistake made by the friends and the adults who were present in the lives of these school shooters was that in processing the verbal cues and behaviors after the fact, many commented they didn't think the shooter was actually planning or capable of committing this act. They often believed it was just an expression of teenage angst or that the teenager was just kidding around.

1.6A AGGRESSORS

The stereotype of a bully is some big, strapping, dumb dude who picks on anyone and everyone because he's bigger and stronger than they are. This stereotype pigeonholes a bully as someone who is unintelligent, has little or no self-confidence or respect (so he must physically get it), and lacks poor social skills and judgment. While this may be true in some instances, it's not typically a true profile of a bully. Bullies can be very socially connected (as is the case with most female bullies). Bullies may do well in school and not even know when they are bullying someone. Unless kids are told that their attitudes and actions make them a bully, they may continue to victimize others.

There are some signs and symptoms that can help you recognize a teenager who's bullying:

Experiences a loss of friends and significant relationships. A bully's friends are always cautious not to get in the path of the bully. They may play the role of toady for a while; but as soon as they're victimized or find a safer relationship, they leave.

Can be more advanced physically, stronger. While it was noted earlier that not all bullies are bigger and stronger, this factor still plays into some common patterns. Since a bully's greatest weapons are power and intimidation, physical strength and size play into his arsenal. As other teenagers start to grow stronger both physically and in character, the bully begins to lose his source of intimidation. This may cause him to move on to more violent means or even intimidate someone with weapons.

Can be hot-tempered, easily angered, or impulsive. A bully is often set off easily. Teenage bullies learn that if they escalate and are given to outbursts of anger, they can intimidate others and control the situation.

Other students may seek him out—until his real colors show. As bullies get older, their popularity fades and others start to reject them. The point to watch for here is who and how others flock around this person. If younger teenagers begin to emulate a peer, then that's who adults should watch. If that teenager is a bully, then he'll act in unkind ways toward many teenagers, who will then choose not to be in the bully's circle of friends.

Appears to be self-absorbed and have delusions of grandeur. Bullies were once thought to be self-abasing and having low self-esteem. The old adage was, "Bullies have such low self-esteem that they have to put others down to make themselves feel good." In fact, that's a myth. Bullies believe themselves to be top dog or queen bee. Often they're very engaging or charming toward adults.

Tends to seek attention. Teenagers who are prone to aggressive behaviors are often disruptive. They can annoy their peers, disrupt classes and meetings by being the jokester, and draw attention to themselves through inappropriate means.

Tends to break or end-run rules and authority.

Blames others or circumstances for their inappropriate behaviors. They typically refuse to take responsibility for their actions.

Tends to see violence and aggression as a positive means to an end. For guys particularly, aggression may be viewed as being manly.

Acts in a dominating and controlling way.

Displays poor social skills and judgment. As they grow older, some bullies lack good social judgment. They seem to opt to use more desperate measures to maintain control. Their judgment wanes as they venture more into delinquent and illegal behaviors, substance use, and more aggressive means by which to control others.

Lacks empathy and care for others. This grows out of the self-centered attitude often found in aggressive and violent teenagers.

Tends to be easily threatened. Bullies tend to interpret threat and provocation from nonthreatening situations, such as innocent glances, comments, gestures, and nonviolent contact. This constant inference of a threat can lead them to justify their aggressive behaviors.

May have a sense of entitlement. Bullies believe the world revolves around them. Some may blatantly present as being very self-absorbed and overestimating their abilities, talents, and skills. They may even have grandiose ideas about the quality of their relationships, even though the depth of relationship is greatly lacking.

Thrives on the response of the victim. A bully is energized by someone's fear. They get pleasure out of dominating and controlling others. They can go to elaborate measures to intimidate because of the rush they get from their victims' fear and pain.

Conversely, when their victims cease to be intimidated, they resort to more elaborate measures.

Needs to have an audience. Some forms of teenage aggression are done in social context. Gangs are a perfect example of aggression being a common threat to the social context, a form of group entertainment, or the means by which the community is empowered.

May have been bullied, threatened, or physically assaulted themselves. They may have been raised in an environment in which violence and aggression were modeled. It's hard to imagine that violence and aggression happen behind the closed doors of our church families, but it does. Some of our teenagers only know aggressive means to solve their problems or manage their pain.

The long-term consequences of bullying behavior compounds. Teenagers who bully are more likely to engage in more aggressive and hostile behaviors as they grow older. This behavior can often include substance use and abuse, as well as lead to committing a crime. Teenage bullies are four times more likely to be criminally charged than their nonbullying contemporaries.[31]

1.6B VICTIMS

At one point it was believed that only the physically weak were bullied. That isn't true. Victims can also be people about whom a bully merely perceives some form of weakness, which can include anything from physical or emotional weakness to being fashionably or culturally out of step. This perception can also be antithetical in that a bully may believe she is superior and, therefore, that anyone can be bullied.

Many teenagers won't disclose they're being bullied. Bringing an adult into the picture threatens their sense of emerging adulthood and erodes their self-esteem. It's imperative that people who care for teenagers recognize signs that may indicate bullying. Realize that younger teenagers are more susceptible than older ones and that even teenagers who seem to have it all together can be the victims of a relentless bully. Here are some things to look for when determining who's being bullied:

A victim relates better with adults and children than their peers. You might find this teenager hanging out with the adult youth ministry leaders more than with the other students.

A victim has few or no peer friendships. She may isolate herself by spending a lot of time at home or in her room.

A victim comes home from school with damaged or missing possessions, clothing, or books. He may also have bruises or cuts he can't or won't explain.

A victim's academic performance may begin to fail. There may also be a noticeable change in productivity and performance in other activities, chores, employment, and even in areas of interest, such as sports, the arts, and so on. This may also become evident in her service in ministry.

A victim may have some health issues. He may complain of ailments such as headaches, stomachaches and nausea, cramps, etc. in order to avoid going to school.

A victim's eating habits may change. When teenagers are worried or afraid, they may begin to eat more or they may lose their appetite altogether. Each individual reacts differently. If there is a change in a teenager's eating pattern, then this may be an indication something is wrong.

A victim may display more fear and anxiety. The teenager may avoid certain routes to school, change her plans suddenly upon finding out that a bully may be present at an event, go to elaborate lengths to rearrange schedules and transportation, and so on. Some teenagers even avoid going to the bathroom all day because that's a place where a bully can corner them. Assess the mood of the teenager when she comes home from school, youth group, or an activity. If she seems upset, sad, depressed, or stressed, then she may have experienced an encounter with a bully.

A victim could experience changes in sleep patterns. Teenagers who face the persistent fear of pain and threat often have difficulty feeling safe and turning off their brains long enough to sleep. Altered sleep patterns can include insomnia, frequently waking up during the night, shallow sleep, and nightmares. Their sleep patterns may also shift noticeably in terms of when and where the teenager falls asleep. Teenagers who have difficulty sleeping at night may fall asleep in the middle of the day while sitting in the living room where there's lots of noise and activity simply because it offers some sense of safety and because they're exhausted.

A victim appears to have low self-esteem. Teenagers who are bullied are persistently beaten down. They may comment on how abnormal they are, constantly put themselves down, demonstrate a self-defeated attitude, and so on.

A victim may seem easily annoyed or provoked. A teenager who feels out of control may bully those who are weaker, such as their younger siblings. They may also be attempting to muster up the fortitude for a confrontation they'll never make. Comments that seem minor and harmless become barbed to a teenager who's in pain. They may lash out in the safety of secure relationships to regain some control over a life they feel is totally lacking.

A victim may withdraw from social situations and relationships. In severe cases, a bullied teenager may become very withdrawn, shy, unpopular, and never assert himself.

A victim may be at risk of committing suicide or homicide. Suicidal and homicidal ideation isn't difficult to detect because there are always verbal cues. Teenagers who entertain these notions make comments such as, "I'd be better off dead," or "I hate her so much, I could kill her." While these may be inappropriate outbursts of venting anger, they also serve as signals something may be brewing. Those verbal thoughts—even when muttered under one's breath or in passing—need to be attended to. They allow the caring adult an invitation into the teenager's pain. If teenagers feel as though their lives are hopelessly painful daily trauma, and if the bullying persists relentlessly without relief, then they may resort to death as a way of escape.

Teenagers who commit suicide as a result of being bullied are said to have engaged in an act of *bullicide*. In a very real way, this tragic event comes at the hands of bullies who can never be held accountable for it. Recent accounts of teenagers who took their own lives because of the overwhelming oppression and elaborate measures of a bully revealed that adults (parents, older siblings, friends) enabled and even participated in the schemes that made life unbearable for the victimized teenager. Our legal system has little recourse right now against such hateful acts.

1.6C GANGS

Gangs are no longer an urban, disadvantaged-youth phenomenon. Teenagers in the suburbs have begun to form gangs. Many police departments across the country—even around the world—have begun reporting gang activity and development among both middle-class and affluent teenagers. The Department of Justice estimates there are more than 20,000 gangs across the United States with more than one million members. The age of gang members ranges from 12 to 25 with a median age of 17.[32] Gangs have broken past economic and ethnic boundaries to become a vehicle for teenage aggression.

Justice organizations tend to agree that a gang is a group of teenagers and young adults who form a strong allegiance—bonding for a common purpose—and engage in violent, aggressive, or criminal activity. Gangs are usually identified by a culture they invent that's unique to their identity, such as having a common language, clothing (colors) and accessories, symbols, values, causes, and so on.

Traditional urban gangs still retain some ethnic boundaries. They congregate in neighborhoods using territorial borders to protect them. Suburban gangs tend to meet in schoolyards, malls, cinemas, public parking areas, and sometimes even church parking lots. Not needing to protect their territory, suburban gangs act violently toward people they don't like or they believe disrespect them.

Urban gangs usually view suburban gangs as wannabe or scavenger gangs. And therefore scavenger gang members (who typically aren't as homicidal as territorial gangs are) run the risk of being killed for their gang involvement if they encounter urban gangs. Some urban gangs sanction suburban gangs, giving them a broader base of operation.

Gangs recruit kids as young as 10 and 11 years old who are known as "could-bes," or potential future members. Junior high and younger high school students who are "could-bes" can hang out with the gang, but they must prove their loyalty by participating in some illegal activity, such as theft, vandalism, or drug running. When a teenager seeks to become a full member of the gang, he engages in a violent rite of passage. This initiation rite (sometimes called getting V-ed in, jumped in, rolled in, or beat in) involves the brutal beating of the initiate by selected gang members. The gang usually defines the boundaries of this beating, including how long it goes on and how and where the initiate can be hit. These brutal beatings can leave the initiate bruised, broken, and bloodied. However, if the initiate survives the beating, he shows a willingness to suffer for the gang and proves his toughness.

Some students are either so attracted to the gang lifestyle or so fearful of others that they'll gladly endure the initiation to have the loyalty, security, and power a gang offers. Some gangs will allow the initiate the option of forgoing the beating in lieu of a mission. This accomplishes the same goals as being jumped in, but the initiate must engage in some violent act against a rival gang member. One common mission is a drive-by shooting.

Girls also seek membership in gangs. Some gangs offer the same initiation ritual for girls to join as they do for guys. But many require that a girl proves her loyalty by engaging in sexual activity with each male member of the gang. Her loyalty and toughness is proved if she willingly does this without the use of protection. Girls tend to have a lower status in a gang, but they join because of the empowerment, protection, and shock value it provides (in other words, they do it to spite their families). There's also been a rise in the formation of all-girl gangs that prove to be just as violent and dangerous as any male gang.

Students who live in the suburbs and the inner city are attracted to and recruited by gangs. Adolescence experts have identified several factors that lead teenagers to join gangs:

Gangs provide status, recognition, and respect.

Teenagers who are attracted to the gang lifestyle need or have a perceived need for protection. Joining a gang can be a teenager's way of expressing his grievances, desires for retribution or vengeance, or a need to be defended.

Gangs provide a sense of belonging. Teenagers are attracted to a sense of loyalty by a group of peers who will "die for you" or "go to war for you." This is reinforced by the fact that personal disputes and attacks become the agenda of the entire gang.

Gangs offer excitement! Gangs provide organized angst, which allows some teenagers the freedom and thrill of rebelling. Some teenagers just need the proper vehicle to validate their desire to engage in delinquent and criminal activity.

Family history. Many times kids join gangs because their older siblings or cousins were members of the same gang.

An adult leader serves as a role model in a gang. The absence of a positive adult male creates a craving in teenagers to find a man who will invest in and protect them—even if it's done in a negative way by leading them into rebellion. Oftentimes the gang leader fills a gap in the teenager's life.

Power. A gang stands as an organized force that defies the authorities of a society. This allows a teenager freedom and power through defiance.

Rejection of parental and affluent values.

Gang membership provides illegal economic opportunities. Material gain comes through drug trafficking, robbery and the sale of stolen items, and extortion, allowing gang members to achieve certain personal freedoms and affluence.

Gangs offer an escape from traditional lifestyles (school, home, church). Teenagers may feel they've been labeled as failures, losers, and so on in these places. So they try their hand at doing something they can be good at instead—aggression.

Gang involvement, particularly in suburban gangs, is secretive. Teenagers don't want to make a big deal out of it until they're a full-fledged member. So how can a youth worker or parent tell if a teenager is involved with a gang? There are a few warning signs:

There's a shift in the teenager's friendships. Teenagers will start to realign their lives with members of the gang.

There's a change in a teenager's standard of living or she has some newly acquired possessions. Theft is a big part of gang involvement. Teenagers involved with a gang often show up with new and expensive clothes and toys.

Graffiti and certain gang symbols are discovered. These can appear on notebooks, clothing, or even drawn (but sometimes tattooed) on the teenager's body.

Weapons may be found. Teenagers who get involved with gangs may begin carrying weapons, such as knives, baseball bats, pipes, brass knuckles, hammers, pipe wrenches, and guns.

Tattoos and brandings (burned symbols) appear on the teenager's body. These marks may appear on the hands, arms, or legs.

The teenager now pervasively and consistently wears a particular color. This becomes more obvious when their friends are also wearing the same colors. Or they may constantly wear the colors and symbols of a professional or college sports team. Team colors, symbols, and initials serve as the socially acceptable camouflage for the gang's colors, symbols, and initials.

Gang members often dress to the right or left. This is indicated by wearing a baseball cap to one side, rolling up one pant leg or shirt sleeve (on the same side), turning up the collar (again, only on one side), wearing earrings or piercings on one side, wearing a single glove to indicate they're dressing to a side, and so on.

These fashion modifications indicate an alliance with gangs. And gangs identify their loyal members in this way. It's important to note that a teenager who begins to dress like this but is *not* in a gang runs the risk of becoming a victim of the gang's violence and aggression.

A teenager begins using special handshakes or hand signals. Teenagers are always messing around and creating new ways to affectionately greet each other. Parents shouldn't be overly concerned at the first sign of an unusual, well-rehearsed handshake. However, this becomes a problem when hand signals are passed to indicate association or when a handshake becomes the identifying mark among certain friends—along with some of the other signs revealed in this section.

A teenager starts to use new sayings or there's an overall change in his vernacular. New words and a linguistic style that has specific meaning to gang members creep into the vocabulary. The linguistic style may also be accompanied by certain gestures that convey meaning and allegiance to a gang.

There's evidence of the use of drugs and alcohol. These substances are often readily available to gang members. One way of proving your loyalty to a gang is to participate in the activities of the gang. Getting wasted may be a common pastime of some gangs.

The teenager has unexplained injuries.

The teenager has frequent run-ins with school authorities and the law.

Once again, it's important to note here that if a teenager is mimicking gang involvement in order to look cool or be perceived as tough, that behavior can be risky and dangerous.

1.7 MYTHS ABOUT BULLYING

Bullying, violence, and aggression are very destructive forces in the lives of teenagers. But because teenagers don't readily let on they're being victimized, the issue can stay hidden. This cover-up can give rise to many myths and misconceptions about teenage violence, hindering any proactive and effective action that can be taken to stop and prevent teenage bullying and aggression.

Most youth workers know that teenage violence is a reality, but they also tend to buy into some of the following myths:

MYTH 1: BULLYING IS ONLY A GRADE-SCHOOL THING.

We tend to believe that by the time a person reaches her teenage years, she's mature enough to avoid the childish name-calling tactics that are associated with bullying. We also believe that most teenage victims have internalized the "sticks and stones may break my bones, but names will never hurt me" philosophy. The truth is that while bullying does decrease somewhat as students mature, it doesn't stop. In fact, bullies become more aggressive with older teenagers in order to maintain control over their victims. Youth workers must be proactive to address issues and create programs that confront teenage bullying.

MYTH 2: TEENAGERS WHO THREATEN MASS HARM (SCHOOL VIOLENCE OR ACTS OF VENGEANCE) WON'T REALLY DO IT.

Teenagers say outrageous things. They may threaten to harm others or sensationalize their angst and rebellion. For most teenagers, this statement is true; but it takes only one teenager to carry out his plans and leave everyone wishing they didn't buy into this myth. Every threat of harm against an individual or a group by any teenager should be treated seriously. Teenagers who make such comments as an attention-seeking ploy or joke should be made aware there are consequences surrounding the things we say.

MYTH 3: MOST TEENAGE ACTS OF VIOLENCE HAPPEN WHEN TEENAGERS SUDDENLY SNAP.

Many times mass violence—or even violence against an individual—results when a victimized teenager reaches the breaking point and commits an uncontrolled act of insanity. While it's true many teenagers reach the breaking point and can no longer handle the pain and agony of being victimized, it *isn't* true that they experience a psychotic break. Most acts of mass violence and even gang violence are premeditated. Weapons are gathered, plans are formulated, and, in many cases, suicide strategies are calculated. In addition, teenagers who act in violent, vengeful ways leave verbal and behavioral cues in an attempt to feel as though they've regained control.

MYTH 4: BULLIES HAVE SELF-ESTEEM ISSUES.

This myth is fueled by the notion bullies harm others so they can feel good about themselves or because they feel so bad about themselves. In truth, many bullies have an attitude of superiority and entitlement. They crave power, love exercising control over others, and believe their actions are acceptable. Many bullies even do well in school and know how to charm adults.

MYTH 5: CHILDREN WITH BEHAVIOR PROBLEMS BECOME VIOLENT TEENAGERS.

Childhood conduct does not predispose an individual to become a violent or problem teenager. The church could be a strong agent of hope in a child's life by not labeling him. Powerful words of love and affirmation spoken into the life of an unruly child can germinate into a transforming agent. In addition, as children mature and their cognition changes, many children with behavior problems shed their bratty ways to become very stable teenagers.

MYTH 6: AFRICAN AMERICAN, HISPANIC AMERICAN, AND URBAN TEENAGERS ARE MORE LIKELY TO ENGAGE IN VIOLENCE.

There is no research that supports this claim. Violence cuts across racial barriers. And while it's true that a cycle of poverty can lead to more aggressive means, that doesn't necessarily translate into violence. Gangs are no longer an ethnic, inner-city phenomenon. Suburban gangs and even all-girl gangs are an ever-increasing issue.

MYTH 7: TEENAGERS WHO WERE PHYSICALLY ABUSED AS CHILDREN ARE MORE LIKELY TO BECOME ABUSERS.

I know of a church that wouldn't let abuse victims serve in their children's ministry because the leaders believed this myth and desired to protect their children. While it's true that most people who are abusers have been abused, it's unfair and unsubstantiated to assume that most people who've been abused will abuse others. Violence is a learned behavior. Some abused people learn to be violent, but many more learn that it's painful and destructive. Adherence to this myth can lead to destructive policies that alienate, bully, and even perpetuate victimization, making the church far from a safe and restorative place.

MYTH 8: VIOLENCE IS A PART OF THE FALLEN HUMAN CONDITION AND NOTHING WORKS TO PREVENT OR CIRCUMVENT IT.

It's true the fallen human condition predisposes itself toward sinful behaviors such as violence. However, the work of redemption is visible in preventative and remedial efforts. There are many effective strategies, programs, and policies that have worked and do work. Some churches measure their success by "growth," meaning numbers. Instead, churches should measure their effectiveness by their impact in the community. For example, if the church were effective in the community, then violent crime should go down. Churches should ask themselves if the community would become more violent if they were no longer in that community. (In section 3 of this book, you'll look at some practical strategies that work against bullying, violence, and aggression.)

MYTH 9: BULLYING DOESN'T HAPPEN IN MY YOUTH GROUP.

The Center for the Study of the Prevention of Violence has revealed that bullying happens more often in environments in which the adult supervisors are indifferent to or tolerant of bullying.[33] Youth groups can be a breeding ground for bullying. This can include popularity issues, power struggles, relational jealousies, and even spiritual elitism. Belief in this myth can cause youth workers to become blind to the hurts of the bullied teenagers who are right in their midst.

MYTH 10: BULLIED KIDS NEED TO LEARN HOW TO STAND UP FOR THEMSELVES.

We must realize that bullied teenagers feel caught in a relentless cycle of torment. Everything from fear to an inability to cognitively work through potential solutions keepz them from getting help. Someone needs to step in. Remember: If you aren't a part of the solution, then you're a part of the perceived problem and reinforcing the bullied teenager's feelings of loneliness, worthlessness, and victimization.

UNDERSTANDING HOW THEOLOGY INFORMS THE ISSUES OF IBULLYING, VIOLENCE, AND AGGRESSION

| SECTION 2 |

2.1 THEOLOGY OF VIOLENCE

2.1A JUSTICE OF GOD

Throughout Scripture, we see the pain and plights of God's people. God's heart breaks over them, yet God allows them. God's people cry out to God for deliverance. Even David, in the book of Psalms, ponders the justice of God through his own agony. We see David's pain and hear his cry for justice against the evil done to him:

- David asks God to deliver him and let the wickedness end (Psalm 7:8-9, 54:1-3, 120:1-2, 140:1-13).
- David feels as if God has abandoned him (Psalm 10:1, 13:1-2, 22:1-2).
- David asks God for justice against those who speak evil against him (Psalm 12, 41:5-9).
- David asks God to fight for him (Psalm 35:1-8).
- David comes to know that God will fight his battles. He concludes that God will deliver him, exact justice, and have vengeance (Psalm 94).
- Later in the Bible, Paul reminds us vengeance belongs to God, so we shouldn't take that into our hands (Romans 12:19, 1 Thessalonians 4:6).
- Jesus teaches that his "New Commandment" way of dealing

with injustice is to turn the other cheek—and trust that God will take care of things (Matthew 5:38-39).

2.1B NEW COMMANDMENTS

Jesus tells us that the greatest commandments are to love God and love others (Matthew 22:36-40, Mark 12:29-31, Luke 10:25-28). Jesus also reminds us that people will know we're his disciples by our love for one another (John 13:34-35). A youth ministry must be marked more by the Great Commandment than by the Great Commission. Our primary task is to challenge students to love. If love marks a youth ministry, then it will be a safe place for victimized teenagers. And bullied teenagers will find healing and restoration there. In other words, it will become a place where hurting teenagers can find acceptance. Loving ministries embrace unlovable teenagers—both the bullied and the bullies. The Great Commandment must be the underlying theological foundation that guides our decisions and strategy in addressing teenage bullying, violence, and aggression.

2.1C GOSSIP

In his epistle to the church, James warns about the danger of an untamed tongue. He compares it to a fire that's ignited by hell itself (James 3:6) and says it's full of deadly poison (James 3:8). Teenagers don't understand the destructive power of their words. Sometimes words can literally have fatal consequences. More than any single topic, the writers of Proverbs talk about the devastating force of unguarded words. The person who gossips, slanders, or spreads lies, is called a fool. Solomon tells us, "The mouth of the righteous is a fountain of life, but the mouth of the wicked conceals violence" (Proverbs 10:11, NASB). Teenagers need to be made aware that contributing to hurtful conversations or communication is destructive and may lead to fatal consequences. We should help our students learn to speak kind words that bring healing and restoration.

2.1D IDENTITY IN CHRIST

Bullying erodes the core identity of a teenager who's desperately working through the developmental task of identity formation. We need to help teenagers decipher and discern the false messages they receive about themselves by continually reminding them how God sees them. They need to know that what God says about them is the truest and most meaningful thing, not what others say or believe about them. A good starting place is in Philippians 1:6, where Paul reminds us God began a good work in us and is still perfecting it. Teenagers need to know that God designed them to be good! And Ephesians 2:10 tells us God made us to do good works.

Here are some other truths about who teenagers are that can help them formulate their identity in Christ:

- You're God's Child (John 1:12, Romans 8:14-15, Galatians 3:26, 1 John 3:1-2)
- You're Christ's Friend (John 15:15)
- You're Chosen and Beloved of God (John 15:16, Colossians 3:12)
- You're an Heir with Christ (Romans 8:17, Galatians 4:6-7)
- You're a New Creation (2 Corinthians 5:17)
- You're Holy and Righteous (Ephesians 4:22-24)
- You're Free from Being Condemned (Romans 8:1, Colossians 1:13-14)
- You're Made Complete in Christ (Colossians 2:9-10)
- You're Approved by God (2 Timothy 2:15)
- You're Born of God, and the Devil Can't Touch You (1 John 5:18)
- You're a Member of Christ's Body (1 Corinthians 12:27, Ephesians 5:29-30)

• You're a Citizen of Heaven (Ephesians 2:19, Philippians 3:20)

2.2 QUESTIONS THAT DEMAND THEOLOGICAL CONSIDERATION

2.2A WHY ARE PEOPLE SO CRUEL?

People are born with a sinful nature—all people! When sin entered the world, it brought pain, suffering, power struggles, hate, insecurity, fear, ignorance, violence, aggression, hopelessness, sadness, loneliness, and desperation. People are cruel out of their selfishness and desire to be accepted, loved, and needed. They may be cruel because of the pain and cruelty that's been heaped onto them. Their cruelty can also be the result of Satan's control of their lives.

People are cruel for many reasons, but the solution is they need a Savior. Those of us who know this Savior may suffer the cruelty and persecution of others, but we can also live in the victory of being saved from sin. As a result Jesus tells us to (1) pray for those who persecute us, and (2) love our enemies (Matthew 5:43-44). By doing so, we show we are redeemed children of God.

2.2B WHY DOES GOD ALLOW SUFFERING?

If God is in control, why does he allow suffering? Why doesn't God just correct the injustices we endure? Why does God allow me to experience so much pain? Teenagers who are experiencing the pain of perpetual bullying, violence, and aggression often ask some form of these questions. The problem of evil is complex. Through the centuries people have tried to understand it and explain it. For a teenager who's in the middle of the agony, not many answers will satisfy.

The best thing to do is let your students know that you don't have a clear answer, but you do know that Jesus endured similar suffering. He was scorned, mocked, abused, ridiculed, treated unjustly, beaten, and bullied to the point of suffering a cruel death at the hands of those who hated him. Jesus understands exactly how that bullied teenager feels. Isaiah calls Jesus a "man of sorrows" (Isaiah 53:3 NASB) and the "suffering servant" (Isaiah 52:13-53:12). Sometimes becoming more like Christ means we'll taste suffering like Jesus did. Yet we know our suffering is only for a season because Jesus suffered in order to free us from the bondage of sin so we can live life to its fullest. There is hope—Jesus promises his followers abundant living (John 10:10).

2.3 SCRIPTURE PASSAGES TO CONSIDER

- Proverbs 1:10-19—Here's a warning not to align yourself with violent friends because their lives will come to ruin.
- Proverbs 12:13—The bully's words will trap the bully, but the words of the righteous people will help them escape trouble.
- Micah 6:8—The good and required thing is that we seek justice, love mercy, and walk humbly with God.
- Matthew 5:3-12—The Beatitudes prescribe a blessing on those who are taken advantage of, persecuted, and reviled.
- Matthew 7:12—Jesus reminds us that we should treat people the way we want to be treated.
- Matthew 25:34-46—Jesus tells us that our true colors are revealed in the way we champion those who are struggling in some way.
- Philippians 2:1-7—Paul reminds believers to regard other people as being more important than they are and to look out for the best interests of others with a Christlike attitude.

PRACTICAL ACTION TO TAKE WHEN IBULLYING, VIOLENCE, AND AGGRESSION HIT A YOUTH MINISTRY

| SECTION 3 |

3.1 DUTY TO WARN

Almost every act of school violence, along with countless other acts of violence, has been revealed prior to its execution. Teenagers who commit violent acts give many warning signs:

HISTORY OF VIOLENCE

It shouldn't come as a surprise to anyone that a teenager who's consistently used overt aggressive behaviors in the past would act out in violence.

PLANNING

Many acts of violence are premeditated and calculated. Teenagers begin planning their violent acts by acquiring weapons, plotting and fantasizing about destroying their enemies, and so on. These plans can often be discovered by adults who have access to a teenager's Web page or by parents who can access a teenager's computer history. They're also revealed in drawings or doodlings on notebooks or in scribbles that exemplify the teenager's angst.

VERBAL

Most times, teenagers will talk about their violent plans. This can come out in various ways. Sometimes they'll make passing comments such as, "I'm gonna kill him," or, "Someday she'll regret what she said about me." While these phrases may just be outbursts of anger and hurt, they're still important warning signs. Another way teenagers express their plans is by asking out-of-the-ordinary questions that reveal an obsession with violence, death, or weaponry. For example, a teenager who plots someone's demise may ask, "Can a person die if..." Cues can also be found in creative expressions of death and destruction in their stories, art, and so on.

If a student is planning to act violently, then a youth worker has an ethical and legal responsibility to tell someone—a duty to warn. This idea grows out of the legal concepts of tort, which are laws that provide remediation for injuries caused by anything from neglect to battery. Under tort laws, civil action can be taken if it's proved a youth worker had prior knowledge of impending violence and did nothing. That means a youth worker can be held liable. Duty to warn requires that a youth worker takes action if she believes harm is going to be done to a minor or by a minor.

A POINT OF CLARITY
Different states have different rules for reporting. Some states mandate that anyone who works with minors must report harm. Other states allow for confidentiality privilege for some professionals, including medical workers, lawyers, and clergy. These privileges often cover required information regarding past events but still hold the professional liable for any harm that's revealed and pending. So if your state allows for clergy confidentiality and you hear a teenager reveal something as confession, the tort laws may not hold you liable. However, if the teenager reveals plans of impending violence, then you must warn someone.

HEADS UP

It may be worth your while to have a conversation regarding these matters with a lawyer in your congregation before you encounter any situation that makes you question your responsibility. Your entire church staff must know the legal parameters for anyone who works with youth and develop the proper protocol for any action that must be taken.

Two questions grow out of the duty-to-warn mandate: "What constitutes harm?" and "Who should be warned?" Let's deal with both these questions.

First, what constitutes "harm" is left to the discretion of the youth worker. The best way to determine this is by simply trusting your best judgment. At first glance, that may seem to be a vague and irresponsible criterion, but let's break it down. If you're in a conversation with a teenager and you begin feeling uneasy about what you're hearing, follow your instincts.

I've had youth workers tell me stories about times when they were creeped out or became slightly afraid or felt the conversation was outside their realm of professional know-how. When this happens, your instincts are usually telling you this isn't normal. Based on your knowledge of and experience with this particular teenager, the normal behaviors and reactions of healthy teenagers, and your assessment of the emotional state of this teenager, you've subconsciously already begun processing the potential of this mentioned behavior becoming real and imminent. So trust your instincts!

The aftereffects of school shootings typically reveal that many people felt uneasy when hearing some of the passing comments and verbal cues, and witnessing the behaviors of the violent teenager. But they dismissed them as merely joking or venting teenage angst. Don't make the mistake of rationalizing away what you feel. It's better to be safe than sorry.

Second, who should be warned? You can start by warning the teenager his words are inappropriate and make you feel unsure about his actions. Many professionals use this opportunity as a time to put a teenager under contract. You simply say, "I want your word you're not going to do harm to yourself or to anyone else." Tell the student you're going to write this statement down and you'll both sign it. Quickly jot down what you heard the teenager say, that he agreed this wasn't a plan of action, and that he promises not to act on it. Then have him sign it. The contract should also include steps the student should take if he feels the impulse to act in violation of the contract. This should include contacting a professional for help; walking away from the situation; engaging in some acceptable activity (running, etc.) to alleviate the aggression. Many times a contract becomes the reality check that draws a teenager out of the fantasy of violence and revenge and into the reality of the consequences of his actions.

The second place a youth worker can go to warn is parents or guardians. Make sure you go with someone who can listen to the process. Tell the parent what the student revealed to you. You may qualify it by admitting that it may just be teenage angst, but it must still be addressed. This may be the opportunity a parent needs to get help for a hurting and desperate teenager.

Finally, you may need to warn the police. There have been occasions when I thought the teenager was serious, capable, and equipped to carry out a violent plan. I was spooked enough to believe something tragic was going to happen. If that's true of your situation, then you should notify police about your conversation with the teenager. You'll probably speak to an officer in the juvenile division who will determine the degree of the threat. His job is to determine the validity of the teenager's plan—your job is to warn.

There may be others in the process you want to warn, such as school officials and employers, who may then notify the police. Remember: Harm against a minor or by a minor is not a confidential issue.

3.2 PREVENTION STRATEGIES FOR BULLYING

By now this book has raised your awareness that bullying is the first step that can lead to more serious forms of teenage violence. You've also become aware you must seek to be a part of the solution, or else you've become a part of the problem. Bystanders perpetuate the injustice and violence inflicted on a bullied teenager by not being proactive. If a youth ministry is going to be a safe and loving community, then it must act to prevent and remedy this huge problem that's inflicted on countless teenagers. Three areas must be considered: The profile and responsibility of the youth group, the health and restoration of the bullied teenager, and the transformation of the bully.

3.2A PREVENTATIVE PROGRAM: THE YOUTH MINISTRY'S RESPONSIBILITY

Programming against bullying doesn't necessarily mean devising a specific activity or teaching, but cultivating an attitude and identity within your ministry. Openly talk about who we are as a people of God—the church. As such we have a responsibility to be a safe place, a community marked by love. And we can develop and build a loving environment in a variety of ways.

Raise awareness among your leadership. Share that by ignoring incidents of bullying, we make the church and youth group an unsafe place. In effect, this helps you evaluate your own ability to create a loving environment.

Be intentional about accepting the unlovable kids. Don't label kids as "unlovable," but be aware there are others who do label them in this way. Make your youth group a place where they're accepted and belong.

Challenge your students to be accepting. You may have to coach them to hang out with each other, come alongside hurting or awkward teenagers, and so on. Give them the vision that *they* make the youth group a loving and safe place.

Teach your students to watch their words. Make sure conversations in your youth ministry always build people up and never tear others down.

Speak directly about and against bullying. Make it your youth group's mission to eliminate this issue.

Challenge students to champion the cause. They can do this by banding together to intervene in bullying situations or by immediately surrounding and supporting the bullied teenager. Bullies love an audience—teach your students to steal the show. Teenagers need to see they can leverage peer pressure by doing the right things during a show of force. Encourage them never to fight or get into a verbal tiff if the bully turns her attention to the group. Just walk away with the bullied teenager.

If teenagers in your ministry are friends with a bully, encourage them to have a talk with that person friend-to-friend and confront the behavior. Encourage teenagers to speak confidently and directly about the bully's behaviors. Help students realize that a bully may dismiss his behavior as fun-loving or just joking around and coach them to confront that type of joking as unacceptable. Help your students rehearse what they'd say to their bullying friend. Let them know that staying quiet makes them part of the injustice.

If direct confrontation doesn't work, then encourage the student to bring the bullying to the attention of an adult. Make students aware that doesn't make them a snitch, but it does make them an advocate for someone who feels helpless and is being victimized.

Ask students to examine their own behavior and choices. Challenge teenagers to walk away from a conversation in which their friends are gossiping about another person. Students should learn that if comments about others are devaluing, disrespectful, hurtful, or false, then they're gossip. Make students aware that judging a person by their fashion, intelligence, oddities, behavior, and even their sin is a form of bullying.

Teach students that as Christians we won't accept the mistreatment of any person in any way. Teach that violence is never an acceptable means of problem solving or a way to get attention and respect.

Create an atmosphere of watchfulness. If there are places in your church where bullying happens (bathrooms, stairways, parking lots—places where adult leaders aren't usually found), have your staff and strategic student leaders frequent those places to create higher visibility.

3.2B IDENTIFYING IF TEENAGERS ARE BEING BULLIED IN THE YOUTH GROUP

Watch for these indicators among your youth group:

Students look upset when they come to youth group. If teenagers become upset during the course of the youth meeting, this could indicate they've experienced a negative encounter at some point during the meeting. Kids can be bullied in bathrooms and parking lots, or while they're moving from one room to another. They may also feel destroyed by other students' hurtful comments or when they're excluded from conversations.

Students isolate themselves. This can be done by walking out of the meeting or moving to the periphery of the room.

Students may complain of physical ailments so they can go home. This tends to be the most effective way for students to avoid being in the same environment as a bully. If that doesn't work, then they'll find excuses to get out of going to youth group altogether.

Students may appear anxious or lacking self-esteem.

Students may lash out at other teenagers and claim the youth group is hypocritical.

Students may appear ruffled. If the bullying becomes physical, the victim's clothing may be messed up or torn, may have minor cuts or bruises, and so on.

Students may be alienated or made fun of by others in the group.

Students may seem distant and resistant to talk to adult leaders. Remember, they might view you as being on the bully's side, especially if you're kind and loving toward all teenagers.

Parents comment about their teenager's dislike of or bad attitude toward the youth ministry and leadership. This attitude may not come across as rebellious to the parent, but rather more apathetic, resistant, or sad.

3.2C EMPOWERING A BULLIED TEENAGER
Before you can empower a bullied teenager to move into a healthy place, you have to identify her. If you've talked openly in your youth ministry about bullying, then it will open the door for you to have a conversation with a student you suspect is being bullied.

Ask the student direct questions. "Have you ever felt bullied?" "When was the last time you experienced bullying?" "Do you feel left out of our group sometimes? Why?"

Encourage all your students not to settle things by fighting or using physical force. Violence is never an acceptable form of problem solving. This will only make matters worse and lead to more violent means of retaliation.

Teach a bullied student that bullies thrive on the reactions of their victims. Coach the teenager to walk away from the bully, ignoring him whenever possible. Help the student do this in a confident way by looking the bully in the eye, standing up straight, holding her head high, and keeping her steps sure. She'll appear less vulnerable this way.

Help the student to break the stigma of victimization by constantly reminding him that what God thinks and says about him are the truest and most important things. God loves and accepts him; holds him in high regard; will never leave him; etc. While all victimized teens need your support in this manner, some may need to seek professional help resolving the wounds bullying can cause.

If the teenager needs to seek professional help, you may need to coach the teen through the process of telling her parents about the bullying. Remember that teenagers don't often want their parents to know because it violates their sense of autonomy. Help the teen understand that their parents must be involved if healing is going to take place.

Encourage the student to be slow to anger. This will be difficult because the teenager is justified in his anger. Acknowledge this and remind the student that the bully is trying to provoke that emotive response. Bullies like to be in control, and the ultimate sense of control is provoking a fearful or angry response from their victim. It gives them a sense of power. If the bullied teenager doesn't get angry, then the bully's tactic is defused. And if the student can somehow inject humor into the situation, then the tables are turned, indicating that the victim is now in control.

Teach the bullied student to set boundaries. This may take time and may require some professional counseling. Some teenagers stay the victim because they're too afraid to confront the mistreatment. As a result they tolerate bad treatment from everyone. Help a bullied student stand up for herself and set boundaries regarding how others talk to and about her.

Have bullied students practice verbally confronting the bully. If they have something rehearsed and learn to say it in a loud, confident way when they're being attacked, the bully will be caught off guard.

Help bullied students regain self-confidence. Encourage them to find and use their talents and skills, become involved in areas of ministry, or engage in some position where they can serve others. Giving students some responsibility within the youth ministry can build their confidence.

Coach bullied students to talk to adults about the situation. By doing this, they'll become an advocate rather than a victim because they're probably not the only ones being bullied by this person.

Help bullied students surround themselves with good friends. This will come full circle if you raise up a group of advocates in your youth ministry who will take a stand against this form of injustice.

3.2D TRANSFORMING THE BULLY
Understand that life-change will happen in the context of

intentionally loving relationships with you and with other teenagers.

Spend time getting to know this student. Be ready to be bullied a bit yourself. Don't tolerate it, but rather keep lovingly pursuing the teenager. Then try to get her hooked up with some very strong and influential students who will love and challenge her.

Help the teenager realize that his actions are causing pain. He may believe his actions were done as a joke or just in fun.

Teach the bully how to manage her anger. Coach the teenager in proper problem-solving skills, conflict resolution, social skills, how to make friends, and how to take responsibility for her behavior.

Suggest acceptable ways for the bully to get attention. Help him understand that violence is never an acceptable form of seeking attention, approval, or respect, and work with him to replace his learned unacceptable behaviors with acceptable ones.

Let the teenager know her bullying behavior will no longer be tolerated. Make sure this is conveyed in a direct but loving manner, and then follow up by pursuing a relationship with her. Don't use this as a way to remove the student from the youth group.

If the bullying teenager fails to see the destruction she is creating; fails to have remorse for her actions; is blatantly manipulative, defiant, or escalates to new levels of antisocial behaviors, threats, and intimidation; then a parent or guardian should be notified and encouraged to seek professional help for the teen.

3.3 HELPING DISORDERED TEENAGERS

Working with students who have oppositional defiance disorder can be draining and very time intensive. These kids aren't outside the scope of youth ministry, and they need the care and attention of loving adults who will build into their lives. You must remember that your role in students' lives is to be supportive. You're not a therapist. If you suspect that a student is having problems beyond what's normal to other students, your first line of action is to refer him to a therapist.

If a defiant student is seeing a counselor, here are some tips for you and for his parents:

- Spend time with the student. Relationship is powerful. This student needs to learn that you love and care for him.
- Keep simple, yet rigid, boundaries. Explain why the boundaries are there and what the consequences will be if the boundaries are violated. Never tell a student he cannot come back to youth group because of unacceptable behavior. It makes the youth ministry and church unsafe places. Rather, explain how it will look if he wants to come back. I always told oppositional students that if their behavior didn't change, they had to come back with a parent (whom I'd notify). Then I'd tell the parent and the student that the parent would sit in back or off to one side of the room and be ready to intervene if there were any disruptions. Disruptive teenagers are working through autonomy issues just as much as nondisruptive teenagers are. So the presence of a parent is a more appropriate consequence than ejecting a student from the youth group.
- Assign one adult leader to supervise and monitor the behavior of an oppositional teenager. A disruptive student can often consume the time of many adult leaders who are trying to care for other students, too. If the disruptive student has the undivided attention of one leader who isn't worried about any

other students, then that student's acting out can be reduced. There are many caring adults in your church who could catch a vision to impact a problem teenager.

- Recognize and praise the student's appropriate behavior.
- Be sensitive to the fact that a student with a disruptive disorder may be bullied by a youth group. Teenagers can become exhausted by or frustrated with the behavior of a disordered peer and alienate him. The disordered teenager may also experience spiritual bullying in the form of judgment and disdain.

You may be called upon by parents who are at the end of their rope with a disruptive teenager. The following are some tips you can give them and draw from yourself:

- Recommend that the family get some professional help from a counselor who's qualified in the area of adolescent issues.
- Avoid power struggles by picking your battles.
- Remember you're always the authority.
- Set reasonable boundaries and consistent consequences. This can best be done when the parent and teenager aren't in the throes of battle. Both should talk through the process and, if necessary, have someone moderate the conversation. Once the boundaries are defined, it's imperative that parents hold the line. Defiant teenagers can erode the parent's patience until they get their way. But if the parent continually shifts the boundaries, then the teenager learns that the boundaries aren't important after all.
- Set a routine and schedule. If an adolescent knows what's expected of her and when it's expected, it can make life more pleasant for everyone. Chores, rules, and expectations should be listed and posted (preferably someplace where other people won't see them, which could humiliate the teenager) so there is reminder and clarity. Teenagers should also know the schedule by the sequence of events, rather than by a rigid timetable. For example, chores must be done before the tele-

vision goes on, or one hour of homework purchases a half hour of video gaming.

- Recognize, encourage, and praise the teenager for making an effort and accomplishing tasks.
- Agree to set a consistent "date." Mark the calendar so the second Saturday of every month becomes a parent-teenager event or outing. This doesn't have to be a big deal (as a matter of fact, teenagers prefer that it not be). Decide you'll go to breakfast or grab coffee—something simple. Once in a while your date can include something bigger, such as shopping, or going to a sporting event. Regardless of what you agree to do, you must enforce some guidelines for this event:

  - This is not a time to evaluate the teenager's behavior or progress.
  - This is not a time for heated discussions.
  - This is a time when you focus on building relationship. Parents can include the teenager in some important decisions they're making, talk about past life experiences and stories, and so on. Teenagers can be encouraged to talk about future dreams or friendships.
  - Avoid looking for teachable moments—this is a time to listen.

3.4 WHAT IF A STUDENT BRINGS A WEAPON TO YOUTH GROUP?

If you're reaching out to teenagers within your community, then chances are a student may bring a weapon to youth group. This is a delicate matter that requires discernment, sensitivity, and good judgment. Many youth workers are quick to confront without first thinking about the ramifications of their actions. Let's examine some discerning factors:

You may not know what's going on in the psyche of this student. Teenagers carry weapons because they're moments away from exacting their vengeance for a life that's been ridiculed. A hurting teenager will most likely misunderstand a confrontation—even when it's done in a loving manner. That confrontation may be the provocation that pushes the student over the edge and sets off a violent response. Teenagers also carry weapons because they're afraid. This incident is less likely to end in tragedy, but it can still escalate.

You must discern the credibility of the source of the information. Most likely another student will be your informant. The credibility of the matter lies in how the student discovered this information. You need to view this situation as a serious issue. If a student says she saw a weapon, then it's much more credible than if she heard about the weapon from a friend of a friend.

A confrontation must be made—but you and your staff aren't the ones to do it. This gets tricky because the police will tell you they need to make the confrontation. If police are called (and this may be the route you must take), then you have no control over when and how they do it. They'll assume and respond appropriately to the worst possible scenario. That means they'll treat the situation as if this student is prepared to go on a killing spree. Therefore, their confrontation may involve a show of force in order to remove the armed student and protect the rest of the teenagers.

However, having the police do so could compromise both teenagers' and parents' perception of safety in your ministry; it could alienate someone who's new to the ministry; and it could create a threatening profile of the church. The police will advise that it's better for you to deal with the angst that comes with debriefing students, parents, and the community after the police disarm and remove a student than to have found yourself in a crisis with dead or wounded teenagers and staff.

The question remains—what do you do if a student brings a weapon to youth group? Here are some steps you should follow:

TAKE PREVENTATIVE MEASURES

Seek out a line of protocol your staff knows must be followed. It would be good for you to contact the local police department and ask them how you should go about dealing with this sensitive issue. Another preventative measure would be not to allow students to bring purses, backpacks, etc., into the building. Have them locked these items in their cars. If that isn't an option, then designate an office where these items will be kept locked away safely. Accompany the teen to that office where she can drop off and pick up her belongings. This will help prevent theft, as well as keeping weapons out of the church building. If a weapon-wielding student is set upon using his weapon for destruction, then your policy will make his plan more difficult. The police confrontation will be much easier and less disruptive when it takes place in the parking lot and not in the sanctuary of your church.

ASSIGN A LOOKOUT

If you believe a student has a weapon and that authorities must be contacted, then make sure another adult always keeps visual tabs on the teenager in question. Police will want to know about the behavior of the student.

CONTACT THE POLICE

It's better to have the police advise you when making decisions that could have violent consequences. You may suggest that the police wait unseen while you ask the student to talk with you outside. This move can prevent some of the spectacle while still allowing the police to conduct the proper search and confrontation. Be aware that if the police are called, they may not let you follow this option.

RECRUIT SPECIAL HELP
Some churches employ security guards or have off-duty police officers patrol the grounds and parking lot during meetings. This can be very alienating and threatening, especially to teenagers. You may do well to seek out someone from your congregation who's a member of some branch of law enforcement to join your volunteer youth staff.

NEVER TAKE A WEAPON FROM A STUDENT
Understand that if a teenager is carrying a concealed gun, then he's committing a crime in many states. In some states carrying a knife is also illegal.

LIMIT THE AUDIENCE
If a confrontation has to be made, do your best to keep other students away. If the event continues without anyone knowing what happened, then you've accomplished this task effectively.

DEBRIEFING
If you must debrief a situation in which a confrontation has been made, assure parents and students that their physical safety is your first concern and that authorities are notified only if there's the possibility that harm may be done to or by a minor.

3.5 WHAT IF YOU RECEIVE A BOMB THREAT?

Youth workers think they'll never experience a bomb threat. We pray this never happens, but it could. So it's important to have a plan of action in case the situation ever arises:

- Take every threat seriously. If a call comes in or a note that mentions a bomb is found, don't second-guess the seriousness of it.
- If a student tells you another student claims to have a bomb, you must notify the authorities immediately.
- If a suspicious device is found (such as a closed-capped pipe, a package that's accompanied by a threat, and so on), don't touch or move it. Immediately notify the authorities.
- Avoid panic. Remain calm and positive. Make sure a few of your strategic adult leaders know what's happening and coach them to remain calm.
- Evacuate the building quickly and in an orderly manner, but without telling students there's a bomb threat. You can tell students you're practicing a new fire-drill procedure in case there's ever a fire in the building. Designate a member of your staff to quickly make sure the building is empty.
- When you evacuate, make sure the entire group is moved far away and to a place where the entire group can be accounted for. It's best to evacuate to a park or the parking lot of another establishment. Make sure students are far enough away from the threat of a possible blast and out of the way of emergency vehicles and workers.
- Make sure everyone is accounted for. Have small-group leaders keep tabs on their students. Have students double-check each other.
- Make your evacuation spot the known place where parents can pick up their teenagers.

3.6 KEEPING STUDENTS GANG-FREE

First off, if you have or suspect that gang members are coming to your youth group, it's important that you make them feel welcome. Treat them with lovingkindness and show them respect.

Second, tell them you respect them and that you expect to receive the same show of respect from them. Gang members usually operate out of a code of ethics, and they respect the church and members of the clergy. If the students in the youth group are kind and respectful toward them, then there shouldn't be any problems. In a community in which there is known gang activity, there should be more concern about teenagers joining gangs than with them coming to the youth group.

Here are some helpful tips to gang-proof teenagers.

- Develop a relationship with teenagers. Every student should have some type of adult relationship. And adults need to know the students well enough to know their emerging interests and who they're hanging out with. Adult relationships also provide a positive role model that teenagers need. Encourage parents to cultivate relationships with their teenagers, too.
- Talk openly about the dangers of gang activity. Make sure your students know about the illegal activities of gangs and the lifelong consequences that come with those activities (some crimes carry life-imprisonment sentences).
- Make students aware they'll lose their individuality, identity, and freedom by joining a gang.
- Dispel the myth that a gang is a family. Families don't require or pressure you to engage in criminal behavior or perform sexual favors, or put you in danger of being beaten or killed. Model what a good family is by bringing the teenager into a loving youth group.

- Discourage students from buying into the culture of gangs (language, dress, activity).
- Encourage them to stay in school. Talk with the students about long-term goals and life dreams. Teach them to avoid the immediate gratification that gangs offer.
- Encourage students to engage in positive physical activity. Boredom can often lead to gang activity.
- Make sure parents are aware of the culture, activity, and values of gangs. In doing so parents can spot and preempt gang attraction.
- Coach students to rehearse respectful ways to decline the advances of gang recruitment.

3.7 PROTECTING YOUR STUDENTS IN CYBERSPACE

Cyber-bullying is a rapidly growing phenomenon. Many teenagers are bullied online and many others cyber-bully—without knowing that's what they're doing. Cyber-bullying plays a big role in bullicide (kids who take their own lives because they're being relentlessly bullied) because the bullied teenager believes the entire world is exposed to the lies, rumors, negative messaging, and so on that are posted about them online. Encourage parents to keep the family's computer in a highly trafficked area of their home where family use can be monitored.

Here are some practical tips you can share with your students to help protect them from cyber-bullying.

- Don't cyber-bully back. It's better not to respond to a cyber-bully. If you respond in anger, you'll diminish any action that can be taken against a cyber-bully.

- Refuse to pass on messages or pictures that aren't positive, have defamatory content or lies, or come from unidentifiable sources.
- Delete suspicious messages from people you don't know without opening them.
- Report cyber-bullies to Internet service providers or Web monitors.
- Cyber-bullies can't always hide behind their anonymity. There are ways they can be traced and held accountable for their postings. In some instances, they can go to jail for their actions.
- Never give out your personal information: Full name, telephone numbers, address, passwords. Never give away your friends' personal information either. If you have personal contact information on your Facebook or MySpace page, consider removing it.
- Don't arrange to meet someone you met online.
- Restrict your friend/buddy lists and keep your photos and communications (including blogs) restricted. What you say online can be revealed to anyone who knows how to get around Web site blocks. Be careful about what you say and post.
- If a cyber-bully threatens to harm you or makes lewd sexual remarks, print or save the communication and notify your parents, school, and the police. If the school is notified, then they can monitor if other students are also being cyber-bullied and notify all of the parents.
- If a profile about you is created without your consent, contact your Internet service provider and have it removed.

RESOURCES ON TEENAGE IBULLYING, VIOLENCE, AND AGGRESSION
| SECTION 4 |

4.1 RESOURCES

4.1A AGENCIES

National Center for Missing and Exploited Children (NCMEC) (1-800-THE-LOST): This organization offers tips on protecting kids from everything from sexual exploitation to a natural disaster. It can provide your ministry with many helpful resources. Check out their Web site at *www.missingkids.com/missingkids/servlet/Public HomeServlet?LanguageCountry=en_US&*

U.S. Department of Health and Human Services, Family and Youth Services Bureau (FYSB): The government provides multiple resources on everything from teenage runaways to domestic and date violence. Access their information from the national Web site at *www.acf.hhs.gov/programs/fysb*

National Runaway Switchboard: This organization provides a hotline for teenagers, parents, and youth workers who suspect a teenager has run away (1-800-RUNAWAY). They also provide other resources such as educational and promotional materials, curricula, and media for parents and organizations who work with teenagers. *www.1800runaway.org*

4.1B ONLINE RESOURCES

www.safeyouth.org/scripts/topics/bullying.asp
The Web site for the National Youth Violence Prevention Resource Center contains articles, best practices, programs, and resources from many reliable and credible organizations.

www.stopcyberbullying.org/index2.html
The Stop Cyberbullying Web site is a comprehensive guide to help parents and students deal with cyber-bullying, cyber-harassment and cyber-stalking. The site explains how to get Internet service providers and law enforcement agencies involved.

www.wiredsafety.com
WiredSafety is a great resource for parents and youth workers. And it extends beyond the topic of cyber-bullying to help teenagers and adults become aware of, prevent, and confront other cyber-dangers.

www.knowgangs.com
The Know Gangs Web site takes a comprehensive approach to understanding and preventing gang involvement.

4.1C BOOKS AND PRINTED MATERIALS

"Love Doesn't Have to Hurt Teens" *(PDF available from www.apa. org/pi/cyf/teen.pdf):* This brochure, written by the American Psychological Association, deals comprehensively and effectively with date violence.

The U.S. Department of Health and Human Services has a Web page ("Youth Violence Prevention") that provides a number of publications that address teenage violence and corollary issues, including school bullying, conduct disorders, violence prevention programs, and others. Check it out at: *http://mentalhealth.sam hsa.gov/publications/Publications_browse.asp?ID=50&Topic=You th+Violence+Prevention*

"Girls Study Group: Understanding and Responding to Girls' Delinquency" *(PDF available at www.ncjrs.gov/pdffiles1/ojjdp/218905. pdf):* Published in 2008 by the U.S. Department of Justice, Office of Juvenile Justice and Delinquency Prevention.

NOTES

1. Tonja R. Nansel, Mary Overpeck, Ramani S. Pilla, W. June Ruan, Bruce Simons-Morton, and Peter Scheidt, "Bullying Behaviors Among US Youth: Prevalence and Association With Psychosocial Adjustment" *Journal of the American Medical Association 285*, no. 16 (2001): 2094-2100, http://jama.ama-assn.org/cgi/content/abstract/285/16/2094 (accessed 3/14/09).

2. (Note: ALL these journal clippings are reproduced as originally written without correcting the spelling, punctuation, or grammar.) Jefferson County Sheriff's Office, *Columbine Documents JC-001-025923 through JC-001-026859*, http://denver.rockmountainnews.compdf/900columbine docs.pdf

3. Cyn Shepard, "Dyland Klebold's Writing," 4-20-1999: *A Columbine Site*, http://acolumbinesite.com/dylan/writing.html (accessed 3/14/09).

4. Jeremy P. Meyer, Erin Emery, and Christopher N. Osher, "Shooter Matthew Murray posted reworked writing of Columbine killer between attacks," *Religion News Blog* (posted December 11, 2007), http://www.religionnewsblog.com/20103/matthew-murray-4 (accessed 3/14/09).

5. Daniel DiRito, "Matthew Murray: nghtmrchld26...In His Own Words," Thought Theater blog (posted December 11, 2007), http://www.thoughttheater.com/2007/12/matthew_j_murray_nghtmrchld26in_his_own_words.php (accessed 3/14/09).

6. Ibid.

7. Jeremy P. Meyer, David Migoya, and Christopher N. Osher, "'YOUR Columbine': Gunman wrote of rejection as reason for revenge," *The Denver Post* Web site (posted December 12, 2007), http://www.denverpost.com/columbine/ci_7696043 (accessed 3/14/09).

8. Dave Cullen, "The Depressive and the Psychopath: At last we know why the Columbine killers did it," *Slate* Web site (posted April 20, 2004), http://www.slate.com/id/2099203 (accessed 3/14/09).

9. Etienne G. Krug, et al., eds., *World Report on Violence and Health* (Geneva: World Health Organization, 2002), 5, http://www.who.int/violence_injury_prevention/violence/world_report/en/ (accessed 3/14/09).

10. U.S. Department of Health and Human Services, Office of the Surgeon General, "Youth Violence: A Report of the Surgeon General" (2002), http://www.surgeongeneral.gov/library/youthviolence/toc.html (accessed 3/14/09).

11. Michael Decaire, "Aggression Types and Criminal Behavior," Suite101.com (posted March 30, 1999), http://www.suite101.com/article.cfm/forensic_psychology/17707 (accessed 3/14/09).

12. Miranda Hitti, "Bullies Target Lesbian, Gay Teens: Study: Homosexual Teens Are Three Times More Likely To Report Being Bullied," WebMD (posted March 30, 2007), http://www.cbsnews.com/stories/2007/03/30/health/webmd/main2630785.shtml (accessed 3/14/09).

13. Amanda Lenhart, "Mean Teens Online: Forget Sticks and Stones, They've Got Mail: Older Girls and Social Networkers Are Most Likely Targets of Harassment via the Internet," Pew Research Center Publications (posted June 27, 2007), http://pewresearch.org/pubs/527/cyber-bullying (accessed 3/14/09).

14. National Center for Injury Prevention and Control, *Youth Violence: Facts at a Glance* (Summer 2008), http://www.cdc.gov/ncipc/dvp/YV_DataSheet.pdf (accessed 3/14/09).

15. National Center for Health Statistics, *Health, United States, 2007: With Chartbook on Trends in the Health of Americans*, (2007), http://www.cdc.gov/nchs/data/hus/hus07.pdf#highlights (accessed 3/14/09).

16. Meghan C. Scahill, "Female Delinquency Cases, 1997," *Office of Juvenile Justice and Delinquency Prevention Fact Sheet #16*, U.S. Department of Justice (November 2000), http://www.docstoc.com/docs/416175/Female-Delinquency-Cases-1997---November-2000 (accessed 3/14/09).

17. Danice K. Eaton, et al., Centers for Disease Control and Prevention, "Youth Risk Behavior Surveillance—United States, 2005," *Morbidity and Mortality Weekly Report—Surveillance Summaries* (June 9, 2006) [55:SS050;1-108], http://www.cdc.gov/mmwr/preview/mmwrhtml/SS5505a1.htm (accessed 3/14/09).

18. Bonnie Fisher, Francis T. Cullen, and Michael G. Turner, "The Sexual Victimization of College Women," Research Report by the National Institute of Justice, Publication No.: NCJ 182369 (2000), http://www.ojp.usdoj.gov/nij/pubs-sum/182369.htm (accessed 3/14/09).

19. Centers for Disease Control and Prevention, "Physical Dating Violence Among High School Students—United States, 2003," Morbidity and Mortality Weekly Report 55, no. 19 (May 19, 2006): 532-535, http://www.cdc.gov/mmwr/preview/mmwrhtml/mm5519a3.htm (accessed 3/14/09).

20. "Graffiti Statistics," Grafitti-Gone.com, http://www.graffiti-gone.com/public/graffiti/graffiti_info.html (accessed 3/14/09).

21. Eileen M. Garry, "Juvenile Firesetting and Arson," *Office of Juvenile Justice and Delinquency Prevention Fact Sheet #51*, U.S. Department of Justice (January 1997), http://www.ncjrs.gov/pdffiles/fs9751.pdf (accessed 3/14/09).

22. For Health Department stats, see Lawrence S. Neinstein, et. al, eds., *Adolescent Health Care: A Practical Guide*, 5th ed. (Lippincott Williams & Wilkins, 2007).

23. "National Runaway Switchboard Statistics on Runaways from Peer-reviewed Journals and Federal Studies," National Runaway Switchboard Web site, "About NRS" link, FAQ page, http://www.1800runaway.org/news_events/third.html (accessed 3/14/09).

24. American Academy of Pediatrics, et al., "Joint Statement on the Impact of Entertainment Violence on Children, Congressional Public Health Summit" (July 26, 2000), http://www.aap.org/advocacy/releases/jstmtevc.htm (accessed 3/14/09).

25. J. S. Vernick, S. P. Teret, and D. W. Webster, "Regulating Firearm Advertisements that Promise Home Protection: A Public Health Intervention," *Journal of the American Medical Association 277*, no. 17 (May 7, 1997): 1391-97.

26. B. Vossekuil, R. Fein, M. Reddy, R. Borum, and W. Modzeleski, *The Final Report and Findings of the Safe School Initiative: Implications for the Prevention of School Attacks in the United States.* U.S. Department of Education, and U.S. Secret Service, Washington, D.C. (May 2002), http://www.ustreas.gov/usss/ntac/ssi_final_report.pdf (accessed 3/14/09).

27. Rosalind Wiseman, *Queen Bees and Wannabes: Helping Your Daughter Survive Cliques, Gossip, Boyfriends, and Other Realities of Adolescence* (New York: Three Rivers Press, 2003).

28. Eileen Poe-Yamagata and Jeffrey A. Butts, "Female Offenders in the Juvenile Justice System: Statistics Summary," Office of Juvenile Justice and Delinquency Prevention (June 1996), http://www.ncjrs.gov/pdffiles/femof.pdf (accessed 3/14/09).

29. *The Final Report and Findings of the Safe School Initiative*, http://www.ustreas.gov/usss/ntac/ssi_final_report.pdf

30. Ibid.

31. Olweus Bullying Prevention Program, FAQs page, "Question: Is Bullying All That Harmful?", http://www.olweus.org/public/faqs.page#Answer_numberCbQ8 (accessed 3/14/09).

32. National Gang Intelligence Center and National Drug Intelligence Center, "National Gang Threat Assessment 2009," http://www.usdoj.gov/ndic/pubs32/32146/index.htm#National (accessed 3/14/09).

33. Dan Olweus, Sue Limber, and Sharon Mihalic, *Blueprints for Violence Prevention, Book 9: Bullying Prevention Program* (Boulder, CO: Center for the Study and Prevention of Violence, 2000).

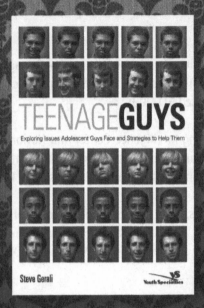

In *Teenage Guys*, author Steve Gerali breaks down the stages of development that adolescent guys go through, providing stories from his own experiences in ministry and counseling, as well as practical research findings to equip youth workers (both male and female)to more effectively minister to teenage guys. Each chapter includes advice from counselors and veteran youth workers, as well as discussion questions.

Teenage Guys
Exploring issues Adolescent Guys Face and Strategies to Help Them

Steve Gerali
Retail $17.99
978-0-310-26985-4

Visit www.youthspecialties.com
or your local bookstore.

youth
specialties